Close, but no Cigar

Six easy steps to solving business problems

by

Ian Woodrow

Illustrations by

Tom Parker

authorHOUSE®

AuthorHouse™ UK Ltd.
500 Avebury Boulevard
Central Milton Keynes, MK9 2BE
www.authorhouse.co.uk
Phone: 08001974150

First published by AuthorHouse 4/7/2008

ISBN: 978-1-4343-3126-7 (sc)

Printed in the United States of America
Bloomington, Indiana

This book is printed on acid-free paper.

For:

Greg
Alistair
Jonathan
Tom
Oliver
Alex
Emma
Ash

You are the apples of our eyes
And our seeds for the future

Preface

All managers, whatever their business, industry or organisation, are expected to be skilled problem solvers. Naturally they are expected to have a number of other skills, but I would argue that problem solving is the least understood or recognised of them all. It is seldom taught at educational institutions and the available literature is relatively scant. How often do recruitment consultants list problem solving as a prerequisite for a particular managerial position, but then fail to test this attribute in the prospective applicant?

Although some people appear to be born with better problem-solving abilities than others, the skill itself can be learnt and developed by those eager to improve themselves in the field. I believe this book will help those that wish to achieve this. It should also prove useful to those who already consider themselves to be effective problem solvers.

CONTENTS

Introduction

He who likes things to be easy will have difficulties; he who likes problems will succeed

– Laotian saying

In trying to come up with a catchy title for this book, I tried to think of how one could describe problem solving in business. No business runs according to plan and if there's one thing you can bank on in the course of your business activities, it's the occurrence of difficulties and problems. Obviously businesses adapt to changing circumstances and it is the manager's job to suggest and implement solutions to the various challenges encountered along the way. Unfortunately, managers are human and are subject to the weaknesses that all of us suffer from in this process (I'll go into these later).

More times than not, the solutions to business problems are sub-optimal and the implementation is half-hearted. Hence the title for my book – business practice, far too often, is characterised by half-baked solutions to the problems that arise. It reminded me of the catchphrase which apparently has been attributed to owners of the hammer and bell devices found in US fairgrounds in the 20th century. With a large wooden mallet, if you thumped a lever with sufficient force to propel a metallic jack to sound a bell at the end of a vertical travel, your prize would be a cigar. Most aspirant strongmen failed the task, but were consoled with the ubiquitous catchphrase 'Close, but no cigar', which we now associate with near success. A solution that falls just short of the target. I might add that the title is also an indirect reference to my method for solving problems!

Perhaps I should explain the focus of the book (i.e. on business). Business activity is the heart of the process through which wealth is created. We recognise that if businesses perform more effectively, a positive ripple effect will be felt throughout society. Aside from the importance of business, it is the field in which I gained all my work experience, and consequently, the one in which I feel most qualified to comment. In my reference to business, I am using as broad a definition as possible. Many of the largest organisations

1

in today's world are government or non-government institutions. I include such organisations in my broad definition of business. But you don't have to be in business to benefit from the techniques described here – they are equally applicable to ordinary, everyday life problems as well.

Business problems are more universal than they are unique or specific. I therefore set out to make this book as applicable to the CEO of a large corporation as to the sole proprietor of a modest concern. I have used the manager as my key role player, but all members of staff, of whatever level, are included. Should it not be incumbent upon everyone in any organisation to assist in the problem-solving process?

The book is set out in three parts. The first deals with the elements of problem solving and looks at the mistakes we tend to make in the process. The second introduces my problem-solving approach (which I have called CIGARS) and shows how to apply it to almost any problematic situation. The third part describes some of the more popular and effective problem-solving techniques and how to use them.

Finally, it is my sincere hope that after reading this book, your views on problem solving will change forever. I trust you'll not only become more effective at solving problems, but you'll experience the immense satisfaction that goes with these achievements. Above all, may you have fun doing it!

Part 1

The Nature of a Problem

If anything can go wrong, it will — Murphy's Law

Everyone knows this cynical maxim, but few would refute it. I once had a book about Murphy's Law listing numerous corollaries and addendums to the original, all of which took a very bleak outlook of the world (*'Murphy was an optimist'* is one that I recall). The book was obviously a tongue-in-cheek view on human progress, but it clearly struck a universal note in recognising that, despite our best efforts, things often go wrong. We always seem to encounter problems along the way.

It doesn't matter what line of business, what type of company, what industry, or where you conduct your activities, problems are universal. Many years ago, when I worked in Scandinavia, our CEO forbade the use of the word 'problem'. He insisted that there were no problems, only challenges. I think he considered the word problem to have negative undertones that would undermine our quest for success. I've chosen to do away with such euphemisms here. But if you're more comfortable with realising challenges than you are with solving problems, I'll be the last to question you.

Why do we always have problems? In today's well-regulated world with tried and tested methods and systems being governed by microprocessors, why do things keep going awry? The answer may lie in the paradox that the more we try to simplify things, the more complex they become. With complexity comes unpredictability, and unforeseen events are the sources of problems.

OK, so what are we looking at?

Basically, a problem is an impediment or obstacle that prevents you from moving from where you are, to where you want to be. We could show it as follows:

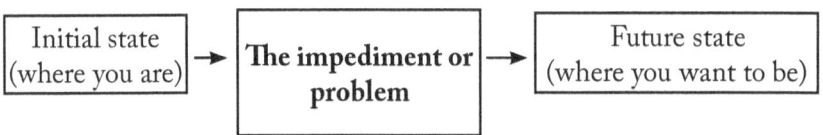

This looks simple enough. In order to move forward we merely need to clear the impediment or move around it. Right?

Unfortunately reality is quite different. We are hardly ever presented with neat little boxes like the ones above. Seldom do we have sufficient background information in order to resolve the situation, and we are often forced to guess and rely on various assumptions (contrast this to hypothetical problems which you find in books or in case studies).

It can be a very demanding and frustrating process where uncertainty, conflict, ambivalence and time pressure can force a person, or a team, into an incorrect decision or action. It is hardly surprising that often the first suitable solution that seems to satisfy the conditions is chosen.

But for now study the diagram above. The three elements are self-explanatory. They are also quite distinct. The better you can understand and describe the above elements of your problematic scenario, the more successful you will be in problem solving. This is not an inherent gift or talent; it is a something which can be learned and improved over time.

Don't fall into the trap of defining your goal in terms of the impediment itself. For example, you are a divisional manager; six months into the year your division is 20% down on budgeted profit. You realise that this unfavourable position has been caused by a significant decline in sales. In six months' time you need to be in a position where the division meets, or exceeds, the annual budgeted net profit.

Let's try and define the elements in this example:

Initial state:	Net profit after six months is 20% below budget
Impediment:	Sales are 25% below the target figure
Future state:	Achieve budgeted net profit by year end

Note that we haven't defined our future state in terms of the impediment or cause. How often do we see managers defining their goals in terms of the problem at hand? In this example declined sales are the problem. So the goal should be to fix this problem. Yes? Let us then say that our goal is to get sales up to the budgeted level at least by the end of the year. Wrong!

For all we know it may not be possible to get sales up to the budgeted level. Perhaps the sales forecast is too optimistic, maybe the market is suffering a cyclical downturn, one of our key customers may have postponed a critical order, and so on. Don't focus on the impediment when picturing your future state. The impediment is something complicating your progress towards your goal; it needn't form part of the goal itself. In this example your desired future state is *the achievement of the division's profit budget by the end of the year.* Although a significant improvement in sales will help, there are other ways of reaching this goal. If we define our future state only in terms of improving the sales situation, we may just overlook these other options.

Wicked Problems

Of course using elementary examples to illustrate concepts is convenient. The real world is not so straightforward and many problems don't have a single impediment which can be instantly identified. In 1973, two urban planners at the University of Berkley (Horst Rittel and Melvin Webber) coined the definition of a *wicked problem* for the more intractable problems that we experience. Wicked problems are those that can't easily be resolved by traditional linear analytic approaches. They are ambiguous, there is no consensus as to what the problem is, they are often associated with strong underlying moral, political or professional issues, they are never totally solved, and the issues with which to address them change with time. Solutions to wicked problems are not true/false or right/wrong, but rather better/worse. I suppose the situation between Israel and Palestine in the Middle East would be one example of a wicked problem.

According to Rittel and Webber, wicked problems tend to have the following characteristics:

- Each time a solution is applied, the problem itself changes. Every applied solution has consequences that can lead to further problems.
- It is often difficult to tell whether the problem has been solved and there are no criteria for determining when the problem has been resolved (i.e. no stopping rule).
- It is not possible to test a proposed (or applied) solution to a wicked problem.
- There is not a well-defined set of potential solutions – the validity of a proposed solution is dependent upon the respective stakeholder involved, who will see it either as worsening the situation or improving it.
- Each wicked problem is unique – lessons from one can't be transferred to another.
- A wicked problem is often the symptom of another problem and it is impossible to identify the root problem of others in the same related universe.
- The causes of a wicked problem, or how they are explained, are numerous and different – these explanations determine how the problem can be resolved.
- Inventive and creative solutions are needed.

- Wicked problems often need to be resolved through the efforts of a group.
- There is no latitude or scope for those resolving the situation to be wrong. The problem solvers are expected to come up with a solution at their first attempt.

This type of problem is sometimes found in organisational change, town or environmental planning, software development or where other societal issues (economics/politics) are involved. Project management, especially if it involves something new within the organisation, is very often the source of wicked problems. It's important that the problem, if it is wicked, is correctly identified as being one. Many wicked problems are not properly identified and as a result get 'solved' in the normal course of business. Unfortunately soon after implementing the so-called optimal solution, the problem rears its ugly head again because it was never resolved in the first place.

If you are dealing with a wicked problem, don't begin by immediately seeking a solution. The secret is to properly understand it and to involve all the stakeholders in exploring the many different facets of the problem. Progress in solving a wicked problem has more to do with understanding the true nature of the situation than advancing to the next stage of trying to structure a problem-solving formula. Discussing a wicked problem amongst the various stakeholders involves learning about the problem and the solution at the same time.

A *tame problem* is the descriptor we use for all problems that are not wicked. However, don't assume that tame and simple are synonymous – many tame problems are very complex. And don't make the mistake of assuming that you have a wicked problem simply because it is difficult and complex. If your problem:

- can be clearly defined
- has a solution that can be assessed in terms of being either right or wrong
- is similar to other types of problems that have been solved in a similar manner
- reaches a definite stopping point (i.e. it is obvious that it has been solved)
- lends itself to analysis and solution through known techniques
- allows for the application of different solutions until a best fit is found

then you are dealing with a tame problem, which is the main focus of this book.

Fortunately not all problems in business are wicked (most are tame), but a fair proportion of them are complex. A single impediment to your situation might not always be apparent and there could be many other underlying associated problems needing resolution. Identifying this array of inter-related problems and their casual links is a critical part of the problem-solving process.

It is very rare to find a problem so complex that it can't be broken down into a series of achievable steps or milestones that can be taken or dealt with one at a time.

Read that last sentence again and never forget it!

Intelligence and problem solving

An intellectual is a man who doesn't know how to park a bike

— Spiro Agnew

We're not about to enter the realms of first year psychology. I'm certainly not qualified in the field and my studies in the subject date back 20 years or more. But a basic understanding of what makes up intelligence is both interesting and motivating to those who suspect that their inability to solve problems is a reflection of their mental capacity.

Before we discuss intelligence, let me deal with a line of reasoning that may possibly be assumed, however subtly, in business today. The first premise of this argument is that intelligent people are good at problem solving. The second is the general belief that managers need to be of above average intelligence in order to reach their level of authority in the hierarchy.

This argument, in the form of a logical syllogism, might be:

All intelligent people are good at solving problems.

All managers are intelligent people.

Therefore, all managers are good at solving problems.

This is an entirely logical conclusion based upon the given premises. But if one (or more) of the premises is incorrect, the conclusion will be false. We can start with the first premise, by asking whether all intelligent people are good at problem solving. The answer is no. To be correct we should have used the word 'some' instead of 'all'. In the second instance we know that not all managers are intelligent people. Unfortunately, in the appointment of managers, there are forces other than mental ability at play. Maybe using the word 'many', instead of 'all', would be more appropriate in the second premise. So what we're left with is:

Some intelligent people are good at solving problems.

Many managers are intelligent people.

Therefore, some managers are good at solving problems.

That's about all we can say at this stage. But to those managers who are not good at problem solving, have faith – you can change! And the same applies to you members of staff planning to impress your managers with your new-found problem-solving skills.

Now that we've shattered the myth of the problem-solving manager, back to intelligence. How do we define it? We recognise that participants on general knowledge TV quiz shows are intelligent (or should be if they're to avoid making fools of themselves). What about people with university degrees? Consider this: the number of intelligent people who never went to university is far greater than the number of intelligent people who did. So a university degree can't be the definitive measure.

For the past number of decades we've measured intelligence according to standard IQ tests where a score of 100 represented the average. If your score for such a test is over that figure, you're considered to be of above average intelligence. But there are as many opponents to the system of IQ testing as there are supporters. Critics claim that the measurement system is biased towards Western scientific thought and then also towards certain competencies. As the renowned anthropologist Stanley Garn once quipped, 'If an Aborigine drafted an IQ test, all of Western civilization would presumably flunk it.'

Nowadays there are basically two schools of thought when it comes to intelligence. The first group believe that there is a single measurable factor that determines all intelligence. This one factor theory is founded upon the high correlation of results from numerous IQ tests. A person who scores highly in one area (e.g. verbal reasoning) is likely to score highly in other areas as well. In layman's terms it's almost as if the scientists are trying to measure the overall speed of one's brain (neural processing speed) and attribute this to a scale indicating general intelligence.

The second school believe that intelligence comes in different forms. The idea had been raised by psychologists in the 1920s, but the concept really only gained impetus in 1983 when a professor from Harvard University, Howard Gardner, published his theory of seven different forms of intelligence. Although the school now has many proponents who all agree on the multiplicity of intelligence, there is no agreement as to the number itself. For example, in his book, *The Age of Paradox*, Charles Handy identifies nine different forms of intelligence. These he lists as:

1. Factual – the ability one has to remember information. People who always do well in the game Trivial Pursuit or in general knowledge quiz shows have a high factual intelligence.
2. Analytical – the ability to understand a complex process. An ability or inclination to solve brainteasers or other intellectual puzzles is indicative of a high analytical intelligence.
3. Linguistic – the ability to easily pick up different languages. Such people have no problem speaking several languages or learning a new one in a relatively short time.
4. Spatial – the ability to see patterns in things. Remember the Rubik cube? Those with a high spatial intelligence could solve it easier than others.
5. Musical – the type of intelligence that allows individuals to express themselves in ways at which we can only marvel. This applies to composers as well as performing artists.
6. Practical – the ability to take things apart, and then reassemble them as before. My father used to describe it as being 'mechanically minded'. Something which, alas, I wasn't!
7. Physical – consider David Beckham with a soccer ball, or Babe Ruth with a baseball bat, or Mohammed Ali in a boxing ring. All were blessed with a high physical intelligence – a superior co-ordination of muscle and mind.
8. Intuitive – the ability to see or suspect things that can't be perceived through the five senses. People who are objectively minded tend to belittle this gift, but perhaps that's because they don't understand it.
9. Interpersonal – the ability to relate well to other people and to use other people in getting things done. The sort of intelligence you'd expect to see in an efficient manager – someone who can inspire his or her team members to perform even beyond their own expectations.

Handy points out that people who score highly on the first two intelligences are those who we commonly recognise as being clever or intellectual. He also notes, interestingly, that such people do not always have a high interpersonal intelligence and this often limits their ambitions. As an example of this he cites Iain MacLeod, a British Conservative politician from the mid 20th century who was described by his rivals as being 'Too clever by half'.

But the interesting thing about this theory is the fact that intelligence has many facets and all of us are blessed with varying degrees of each. A genius in one area can be a relative dunce in another. Obviously a high analytical intelligence implies a good problem-solving ability, but a person who is not strong analytically can still learn to become competent at problem solving through technique and practice. The same goes for other forms of intelligence. For example, I have no doubt that if I consistently played tennis every week with skilled opponents, my tennis-playing ability would significantly improve (to the point where I could give my son a good game!). And from experience, I also know that your problem-solving ability will get better as the number of problems you tackle increases.

Why we find problem solving so difficult

The mind of man is more intuitive than logical, and comprehends more than it can coordinate

– **Vauvenargues**

The vast majority of us struggle with problem solving – why is that? We have a strong natural desire to solve problems (witness the recent Sudoku craze in the Western world) and normally we tend to embrace problems rather than avoid them. It's just that our solutions are not always the best ones. Current scientific opinion would have us believe that the human mind is the most superior computing machine known to man. Why then is it not so effective in solving problems and why are the solutions we choose so often the wrong ones? In a later section I will address the last question (i.e. the mistakes we commonly make when trying to solve problems). But for now I want to look at the way we think and why it is that we struggle with problems.

Effective problem solving requires structured thought. This means that we need to consider all the elements of the problem in a methodical and logical fashion. When we first learn of a problem, our minds typically jump ahead to the possible solutions. We seldom take the time to study and understand all the factors that confront us, and consequently the chances are good that our final conclusions may be flawed. Many brainteaser puzzles, or conundrums, rely on this very human failing in tricking their subjects.

Problem solving, especially of complex situations, is something that we tend to avoid or postpone once we realise that an easy solution is not apparent. Perhaps we hope that the problem will disappear if we ignore it. Maybe there are risks involved in applying a particular solution and we don't wish to rock the boat. But mostly we delay because many problems are frustratingly difficult and require the application of deep thought.

Try getting a group of people to follow a sound structured approach to a problem. You're more likely to encounter glazed eyeballs than passionate enthusiasm. Nobody seems to have the patience to debate the various elements. There's always too much pressure to identify the solution to a problem that is clearly self evident and so move on to the next issue. Am I being cynical? I don't think so. I've experienced the same, time and time again, across four continents and for close on 30 years. And from this I've come to realise that the average human mind is simply not programmed for an ordered systematic approach.

Instead we are hard-wired to act intuitively and impulsively. Here are but a few of our worst traits in this regard:

- Disregarding an alternative proposal when it opposes our own proposal.
- Focusing on conclusions and possible outcomes before a problem has been correctly identified and analysed.
- Failing to think objectively due to emotions around a particular issue.
- Allowing our prejudices and biased assumptions to influence our thinking.
- Accepting the first emerging pattern from a set of circumstances as established fact.
- Refusing to stick to a structured pattern of thinking. The mind feels hemmed in with a formulaic approach and prefers to roam free believing that its random wanderings will result in an optimal solution.
- Scepticism regarding any theory or technique that is quantitative in nature.

In short our minds are ill equipped to think in a structured fashion. Analytical thought, for most of us, goes against the grain of what we're comfortable with. We struggle to keep an open mind for a great length of time. We are quick to jump to conclusions especially when we can detect patterns or indicators of past experiences, or cause and effect relationships.

Your mind is a runaway train. Think about it. When do you allow or instruct your mind to simply rest? We sometimes say that our mind's 'a blank', but this is never really true. Maybe our minds rest when we're asleep, but even this can be argued. When we're conscious, our minds are constantly focusing on some concept or event. There is an incessant buzz of activity. Our minds are machines in perpetual motion. It should come as no surprise that we jump to conclusions in the way we do. Even before a problem is properly formulated, we're working on how the solution is going to be implemented.

One of our greatest shortcomings is our tendency for bias. We will seize any information or data that is consistent with our biases and reject any information that is inconsistent with them. But we won't admit to having these preconceived views. In his book, *The Thinker's Toolkit*, Morgan D. Jones says, 'Humans are only logical in a superficial sense – at a deeper level we are systematically illogical and biased.'

In a later section he describes a mindset as, '...the summation or consolidation of all our biases about a particular subject'.

Most of humankind's achievements have been built upon the experiential problem-solving method of trial and error. This is so ingrained in the human psyche that today we're sometimes encouraged to make mistakes on the grounds that we learn from them. Of course this is true, but it can come at a high cost. Why opt for the trial-and-error method if a little thought at the outset can avoid wastage? Well, one reason is that we're lazy. We tend to avoid effort and resist those things that we find difficult. It's much easier to rely upon our judgement!

Some may point to Malcolm Gladwell as a leading advocate of this fast-track approach. In his book entitled *Blink: The Power of Thinking Without Thinking*, he gives numerous examples of what he refers to as rapid cognition. He distinguishes this from intuition, claiming that the latter tends to be based on emotions which may be irrational. Rapid cognition (the correct assessment of a situation in the first two-second encounter) is, according to Gladwell, quite different from an emotional or gut-feeling approach and in most cases is very rational. Certainly the cases that he describes seem inexplicable and supportive of his view.

Unfortunately not all of us are instantly struck with the correct course of action the first time we perceive a complex problem. I think we need to recognise that it is sometimes *possible* to perceive the truth surrounding something in a flash, but we should not let this be our golden rule. I believe in the power of intuition and I suspect this ability varies greatly between individuals and perhaps genders. Whether you use the terminologies of rapid cognition, intuition, gut feel, common or sixth sense, my advice would be that you only *check* your final decision using this gifted insight after you have carried out a structured thinking approach like the one described in this book.

Close, but no cigar
Why solutions to business problems often miss the mark

Some problems are so complex that you have to be highly intelligent and well informed just to be undecided about them

— Laurence J. Peter

I've entitled this section as I have the book itself, but you shouldn't infer that this is the key chapter or the essence of the book. I merely want to show why problem solving in business is frequently ineffective. It is important that you are able to recognise the common mistakes that we make when trying to solve problems. If you are headed down the wrong path, one of the first things you need is a warning indicator pointing out your error. So as a guide I have tried to include the more common errors (certainly the ones from my experiences) that managers make when working out solutions to their problems. I'm sure many of them will be familiar to you. I've been guilty of a few of them on several occasions.

Mistaken identity
The most fundamental error in problem solving is the one where the problem is incorrectly identified. If a solution is formulated and implemented, the result is wasted time and effort since the underlying problem is likely to remain unaffected. A classic case of this occurring is where symptoms are perceived as problems; in many cases a result of insufficient thought being applied when analysing the problem.

An example of this might be:

Situation:
1) The company's sales are way below the projected targets.
2) The sales team is not active in seeking out new or repeat business.
3) The sales team is demotivated and incompetent.

Conclusion:
The sales team is the problem. We must replace them with people who are capable of carrying out this function.

This may seem amusing to some of you, but it's actually a case from my past work experience. The management team of the company firmly believed that their poor sales stemmed from the inabilities of their sales staff. Their solution was to dismiss the sales team and hire a competent one in its place. This decision was never taken and maybe just as well, since this would probably have been an instance of the symptom being addressed rather than the underlying problem.

Perhaps the managers should have asked; if the sales people are demotivated, what is the cause of this? Are the sales budgets too ambitious? How do our sales people plan and carry out their daily activities? What distracts them from focusing on selling our product? What are these distractions and how can we avoid them? How can we assist the sales people in the performance of their duties? Things in this world tend to be caused by other things. Make sure that the one you consider to be the root problem is not merely a symptom of something else that you can control or influence.

There are other causes for mistaken identity. These include:

- Incomplete information – a decision is taken before enough information about the problem has been gathered or discussed. Critical gaps in the background analysis can seriously affect the type of decision taken.
- Previous experience – a problem appears to be similar to something previously experienced. The same solutions that were successful with the prior problem are implemented again. But this time they don't work.
- Too close to the problem – often described as being unable 'to see the wood for the trees'. If you are too immersed in the details of the situation it can be difficult to take an objective view of the overall problem. This can result in mistaken identity or frustration in not being able to agree on what is at fault.

- Jumping to conclusions – as mentioned earlier, the tendency people have to immediately focus on the possible outcomes before the initial situation has been properly presented or discussed. The human mind needs to find explanations for everything (even if those explanations are inaccurate).
- A wicked problem that was 'tamed' with a problem definition that conveniently concealed the wicked nature of the complication. The solution, from the subsequent linear problem-solving exercise, failed to address the underlying issues. Remember, you can't treat a wicked problem as just another problem!

DEI (Dreaded Emotional Involvement)

One of my professors at business school used this description to caution us whenever we were considering alternative solutions to business problems. He described it as an emotional link to the issue at hand and one where these emotional factors can cloud or influence our judgement in deciding a suitable course of action. This can be very difficult to prevent in practice.

I'm sure many of you will have experience of this in your work lives. Not many managers tolerate their subordinates questioning their decisions especially if their choices appear to be founded on emotional factors. It's a very sensitive point and subordinates recognise that questioning their managers may very lead to their dismissal or at least undermine their career prospects.

A further complication is that DEI is hardly ever overt since those taking the decisions go to great lengths to justify their preferred solutions. Nowadays, with pressures for good corporate governance and accountability, managers ensure that they can demonstrate a number of good reasons to support their decisions. For example, assume that top management is considering a relocation of the company. Naturally a number of factors are taken into account (e.g. rentals, neighbouring facilities, transport for staff, access from highways, proximity to airports, building availability, etc.). One important, but unspoken consideration – how close the preferred relocation will be to the senior managers' homes – always seems to escape attention. That's DEI for you.

Of course there are managers who are quite entitled to make emotional decisions. What about the sole proprietor, or the Chairman who holds most of the company's share capital? It would hardly be our place to question them when they make a decision since everyone is free to dispose of their assets as they see fit. Actually, arrogant or autocratic people are probably more inclined to be victims of DEI than those of a more egalitarian slant.

But even despots should be concerned about making a correct decision, as efficiency is beneficial to us all.

The instances where managers or people in authority exclude themselves from participating in a decision due to their lack of objectivity are rare. This does not mean to say that in every case where a manager has some emotional involvement, he or she should stand down from selected decisions. Without going into the area of business ethics, I think a manager should try to recognise DEI and the possibility it could have in favouring an individual or group of individuals instead of the whole organisation. Always look to see whether those close to the problem have any emotional ties.

Groupthink

Some management teams are characterised by individuals who think along similar lines. The members may be docile lackeys all aiming to please, or not challenge, their dominant leader (it still amazes me how often this happens). Or it might be that, as managers, they perceive themselves as being special or separate from the rest of the organisation. These little elite clubs are swayed by their own perceived importance and their *esprit de corps* leading more to unanimity than it does to disagreement. This like-mindedness, known as groupthink, can be dangerous even to the extent where the qualified view of an outsider is ignored if it runs counter to the group's view. This can lead to disastrous results. The injudicious invasion of Iraq by coalition forces of the United States was a fairly recent example of this. The decision to invade the country was largely based on intelligence reports regarding Iraq's capacity to manufacture or acquire weapons of mass destruction. The inaccuracy of those reports was attributed to a collective groupthink on the part of the US intelligence community.

The longer a group works together, the higher its cohesiveness, and the greater its tendency for groupthink. But it's not that difficult to negate its influence. Include outsiders (consultants, experts and other departmental members, etc.) in your problem-solving group. Make sure that these are people whom you can trust to be impartial, and encourage them to speak openly.

Ego of the individual

All of us have known the manager who believes that his intelligence, education or experience equips him better than any of his colleagues or subordinates to solve the problem at hand. Frequently this confidence is almost understandable, as the manager seems to have a natural analytical ability. But arrogance and self-reliance can lead to a huge ego, which, in turn, can be a difficult and frustrating obstacle. From my experience, I would say there are at least as many managers with ego issues, as there are without them. Ego managers dislike being challenged especially in a group situation. They might even stoop to choking off a potentially effective solution because it was not their own.

There are also those managers who pride themselves on quick, firm decisions. We all recognise indecisiveness as a weakness, but this does not suggest that its antithesis is always a good thing. There are instances when more time is needed to collect and comprehend the facts in a scenario. Sadly a manager with an ego founded on decisiveness may not allow such dilly-dallying. Just remember that quick decisions under pressure are more likely to be incorrect. Time is needed to properly gather the facts, define the problem and assess the various alternative solutions.

Don't let individuals' egos prevent you from getting valuable inputs from others.

In my many years of working in South Africa, I have encountered another ego-related trait, particularly amongst Afrikaans-speaking males. Known colloquially as, *'n Boer maak 'n plan* (a farmer will improvise), this maxim is more a belief in one's ability to resolve any situation due to one's cultural heritage. Although it enjoys a foolproof status amongst its proponents, it is all too often the source of half-baked schemes and Heath Robinson-type solutions.

Living with the problem

Many years ago, in the early days of my work career, I hung a framed saying on my office wall to vent my exasperation. It read:

A manager will sooner live with a problem he can't solve, than accept a solution he doesn't understand

-Anon

I forget where I originally read this somewhat cynical statement (or who quoted it), but I've found it to be quite true. At the time I was frustrated that my superiors were prepared to continue with the company's established work practices although I had identified new methods and techniques that would have saved the company time and money. My enthusiasm for elaborate operational research techniques was only exceeded by my naïveté, and I couldn't understand why others in the company, who didn't follow all the computations, were unable to simply accept that I knew what I was talking about. What I didn't realise was that, in order for people to accept something, they need to understand and appreciate its benefits. Few will buy into your solution simply on the strength of your say so – even, as I found in subsequent years, if you happen to be the boss!

I mention this here, as it was my first experience of a manager preferring to live with a problematic situation rather than trying to improve it. There are other reasons for this curious habit. Very often a proposed solution implies a significant change to the organisation. People may lose their jobs or get reassigned to other tasks. There may be the cost of additional training, expenditure in new capital equipment or in other assets. All of these changes imply risk. What if we don't achieve the desired results? Can the whole scheme backfire setting us further back than we are right now? How will our customers/suppliers/staff react to the change? Why upset the status quo? There can be many consequences to consider in a planned organisational change. A manager is all too aware of these risks when the downsides will reflect on his or her decision. Consequently, it might be easier to live with the problem rather than risk rocking the boat too much. Either that or another solution (less risky, but also less effective) will be chosen.

Problem solving in real life is a fuzzy business. Unlike problems that you find in books or in exams, there is no reference at the end of the book where you can check for the right answer. Nobody can say either beforehand or afterwards what the right solution is or was. Since this is a grey zone, many managers prefer to reduce the effects of the problems they encounter instead of tackling them head on. How many times have you heard the description 'unavoidable occupational hazard'? Who made it an unavoidable problem? All too often people (especially those new to the industry/business) are dissuaded from attempting to resolve a situation by those who 'know better'. No doubt there are some aspects within some industries where one might be hard pressed to develop a significant improvement, but in most cases it is just managers learning to live with their problems.

Time available

As the world becomes increasingly complex, we find less time available for the tasks of each day. Time, like money, is a limited resource and all managers search for time-reducing ways of reaching their destinations. When problems occur there is naturally pressure to find a solution as soon as possible. Since delays are perceived in a negative light, there are those who feel that a sub-optimal solution implemented earlier is better than a more thorough solution at a later time. Of course this is true and it is the task of management to use its discretion to judge which option is preferable. Yet in many cases managers tend to go for the soonest available solution that seems to satisfy the conditions. The result is a half-baked solution that lowers the heat in the kitchen, but fails to put out the fire. Very few problems demand an instant solution – a good job takes time.

Weak management

It is customary in business, when encountering a problem, to call a specific meeting to discuss and resolve it. But running a problem-solving meeting requires certain skills and a different agenda from the everyday business meetings. A climate that gives all ideas and views an equal platform needs to be created. Invariably the strong personalities dominate proceedings so much so that more subdued members feel 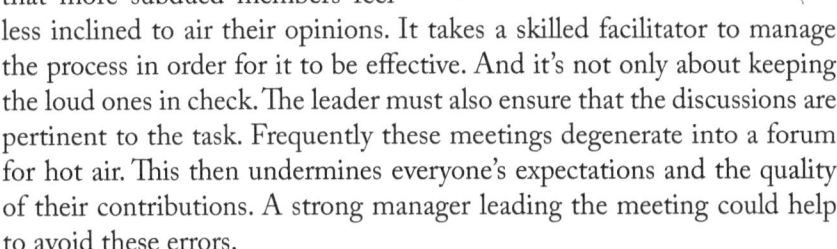 less inclined to air their opinions. It takes a skilled facilitator to manage the process in order for it to be effective. And it's not only about keeping the loud ones in check. The leader must also ensure that the discussions are pertinent to the task. Frequently these meetings degenerate into a forum for hot air. This then undermines everyone's expectations and the quality of their contributions. A strong manager leading the meeting could help to avoid these errors.

Weak management can also contribute to ineffective problem solving in another way. Analysing a problem and developing an appropriate solution is only half the story. Nothing will happen until the chosen solution is effectively implemented. This brings to mind the time I worked for a firm of management consultants. It was a very stimulating work environment and we dealt with a wide variety of businesses and industries. In most cases our clients called us in to address the key challenges they faced. Our assignments basically came to an end when we submitted our final report, which in a way was like providing the solution to the problem. Often we never knew whether our suggestions and proposals were implemented. We liked to assume that we had provided a valuable service, but I think we all suspected that many reports were never followed up with concrete action. A problem will only disappear when the solution is implemented, not when it is discovered or thought up.

Many managers choose to avoid confronting issues especially when it involves challenging the status quo in the company. Organisations are complex societal structures and there are many submarines lurking beneath the smooth veneer of their public surfaces. A malleable manager may not detect the hidden agendas of his or her staff. Even if these covert interests are known, the manager may choose to avoid head-on confrontation if the staff and their experience are valued above the benefits of the resolved problem. Sometimes maintaining a problem safeguards the jobs of some people. Where solving a problem is against the interests of a group of people, don't be surprised if this group successfully reduces the problem to a level where its effects are not immediately apparent. Needs must when the devil drives!

Laziness and apathy

People are naturally lazy and, like electricity, tend to follow the path of least resistance. Solving problems requires a particular discipline and the application of structured thought. A lot of people simply could not be bothered with an exercise that requires such effort. They are more likely to accept any solution that seems to address the problem at hand.

Very few companies or organisations are blessed with a staff complement that generally perceives the business through the eyes of a shareholder. The number of apathetic people in a typical organisation tends to outnumber those that are brim full with enthusiasm and initiative. And solutions to problems in business are not the sole domain of managers – ideally they should come from staff members more so than from managers. If the entrepreneurial spirit in your company has been dashed – if people don't see a direct linkage between new ideas, solutions or concepts – you can expect many of the solutions to problems within the business to be simple quick fixes and stop-gap measures.

Our thinking minds

I was a freethinker before I knew how to think

– George Bernard Shaw

Most of us are aware that the main section of the human brain is divided into two hemispheres each with separate tasks. The left hemisphere is said to control the right-hand side of the body and vice versa for the right hemisphere. This allows people like myself to boast that only left-handed people are in their right minds! Popular psychology holds that the left side of our brain is responsible for logic and the right side for creativity. Some characteristics associated with each side are summarised below:

Left-brain behaviour	Right-brain behaviour
Logical sequence	Random
Reasoning	Intuition
Flowchart to reach goal	Fluidity to satisfy goal
Figures and words	Pictures and images
Describes using words	Needs to mix words & visuals
Seeks and follows rules	No importance on rules
Focuses on details	Focuses on big picture
Scientific thought	Religion and philosophy
Risk averse	Risk taker
Reality and facts	Imagination and fantasy
Follows plans	Follows emotions
Objective	Subjective

Our left brain approaches problems by beginning with the details and then proceeding in a linear fashion. It looks at each element in turn with the aim of arranging them into a logical sequence that will ultimately explain or lead to the desired outcome. For example, a person who has just been imprisoned contacts a lawyer for assistance (assume they have never met before). The first thing the lawyer needs to do is get to grips with facts of the case. She tells the client to start at the beginning and she gets him to relate every detail step by step. While she is actively listening (now and then with the odd question for clarification), the left side of her brain is sorting all the details into a logical sequence. She needs to understand how and why all the events took place so that she can thereafter resolve or defend the outcome (i.e. her client's predicament). During all of this, the right side of her brain is probably in holding pattern.

We like to classify people (as we do pretty much everything) into two categories: right-brain or left-brain thinkers. If we saw the lawyer in action, we might assume that she's a left-brain dominant person. She certainly was following left-brain thinking when performing the case analysis. But is that all she's capable of? Would it surprise us to learn that in her spare time, the lawyer is an accomplished artist? Yes, it probably would, since the thinking one needs to be a successful artist is quite different from that needed to be a good lawyer. We suspect that people will take up careers that fit the type of thinking with which they are most comfortable. We tend to associate unfettered thought with an artist, and we assume that a person who was so inclined would find the daily rigours of a lawyer's life intolerable.

There are elementary tests that you can take to establish whether you're a left-brain or right-brain person. In my case, most of the results indicate a right-brain inclination, but I also have test results that show the opposite. At university, I majored in quantitative subjects – an indication of a left-brain bias, and I began my career in financial management. But I would attribute more of the successes in my later career to right-brain thinking than I would to left-brain analysis.

What we need to find is a balance between the two. Just because many of us seem to prefer one type of thinking to the other, does not mean that its opposite is out of our reach. If you are a 'left-brain' person, there are numerous exercises that will stimulate the right side of your brain, and vice versa. It's important that you develop an ability to think in these two different forms since many problems in real life require the application of thinking from both sides of the brain. If you can learn to switch your thinking between your left and right brain while maintaining an impartial view of the events, you'll become a whiz at problem solving.

With reference to my jibe in the first paragraph of this chapter, being left-handed does not automatically imply that one is right-brain dominant. Studies have found an occurrence of left-handedness amongst artists (predominantly right-brain) that seems to go beyond the 10% probability of being left-handed in the general population. But a direct link has not been proven and many right-brain dominant people are in fact right-handed.

Convergent and divergent thinking

If we take all the elements of a situation and analyse them in order to focus on what the fundamental issue at hand is, we apply what is known as convergent thought. We converge or move towards one point. Under convergent thought, there is only one correct answer (e.g. who was the first man on the moon, what is the square root of nine, etc.). Much of mathematical or scientific thinking can be described in this way. One reason why standard intelligence tests come under criticism is because they only seem to measure this type of thinking. When we use convergent thinking, we analyse and integrate the given or stored information (memory) to a set of circumstances, narrowing down all the options to arrive at the one logical solution.

Divergent thinking is the opposite. Here we begin at a single point and branch out in different directions in a quest for alternative solutions. It assumes there are many answers and it encourages the mind to think freely and creatively – to consider the impossible in a world with no rules. So whenever we take a broad view of a situation in order to see whether there are any other relevant factors to consider, we are thinking divergently. If you were asked to list as many possible uses for a paperclip (or a brick, an alarm clock, a soccer ball ….) you would apply divergent thought in generating your answers. Such exercises are good practice in developing your ability for divergent thought.

By now you will have seen the similarity between left brain and convergence on the one hand and right brain and divergence on the other. Both types of thinking are needed in problem solving. When needing to identify the critical factors affecting a situation, convergence is the effective mode. Where a new or innovative solution may possibly resolve a deadlock, then divergence will provide the answers. The lesson here should be balance – place an equal value on each type of thinking and recognise the circumstances when each is relevant.

Part 2

Solving Problems with CIGARS

I keep six honest serving men, they taught me all I knew: Their names are What and Why and When, and How and Where and Who
— **Rudyard Kipling**

Now that we've briefly considered problems and how they are often dealt with in business, I want to introduce a basic problem-solving approach that you can apply to almost any problematic situation. To some it may seem a little rigid and prescriptive (the design of a left-brain?), but I assure you this is just a first impression. I turned my method into an acronym, CIGARS, where each letter stands for a separate element in the problem-solving process. I normally hate mnemonics, but they're very effective when it comes to recall and application. The great thing is that once you have learnt CIGARS, and more so, practised it, you'll never forget it. In the future, when faced with a difficult problem, simply take each letter in turn and, '…keep your head when all about you are losing theirs….', – to borrow a line from the esteemed writer above.

I have mentioned above that CIGARS can be used to solve almost any problem. Anyone with experience in problem solving might see this as a bit of a rash claim. There are many problem-solving techniques (see Part 3) and all are useful at different times for a particular purpose. CIGARS is certainly not a universal method for solving problems (if such a thing exists). But to solve a problem effectively you need to think in a structured manner. However obvious this may seem, I can assure you that it's not the norm when problems are handled in the business world. And if it takes a simple and elementary mnemonic like CIGARS to rectify these ineffectual and annoying practices, then so be it!

Here's what the letters in **CIGARS** stand for:

Circumstances – what are the facts of the scenario?

Impediment – what is the key obstacle preventing you from being where you want to be?

Goal – or desired outcome, where do you want to be?

Alternatives – what are the ways of resolving or avoiding the impediment?

Review – the alternatives and evaluate each for its effectiveness

Select – choose one (or a combination) of the alternatives and implement.

C – Circumstances

In order to tackle a problem you need to understand it properly. You have to acquaint yourself with as many relevant facts as possible. But this has to be done in an objective and unemotional manner. In many instances when a problem is debated, tempers flare, people become defensive and objectivity flies out the window. On the other hand there may be no debate – people often know that below the surface there are holy cows that can't be challenged and are reluctant to speak out. As a result the focus is placed on the proposed solution. Can everyone live with it; will the cost be acceptable; what will be the effect on the status quo? More often than not, the so-called solution will not address the core problem and there are few people who are prepared to point this out.

But let's assume that you are not one of these political players and that you sincerely wish to get to the root problem and resolve it. One of your first steps will be getting rid of all the clutter. This is by no means an easy task and it requires a fair degree of discernment and open-mindedness. As mentioned earlier, real life does not present its problems as brainteasers with all the underlying elements succinctly described. Most of the information needed to tackle the problem is unknown. There may be many professing to know what these missing pieces are, but it is up to the manager to bring a balanced view to properly assess the true circumstances.

Only the key facts, not the emotions

Our objective here is not to identify the problems or the solutions – we are simply trying to gather the facts without prejudice. Forget everything you've assumed with regard to a particular subject and try to regard it as if you were observing it for the first time. Don't readily accept the opinions of others. Sanitise all statements and views of their emotional content or inherent bias. Place more emphasis on what you observe rather than on what you are told. Try to get outside views, especially those that seem to challenge the in-house opinions. At the same time, beware of too much information. Not only does this take time to obtain and categorise, but also it can lead to paralysis by analysis – a situation where one fails to act due to the complexity of the information or data being considered.

When considering the circumstances follow these rules:

- Stick to the facts and keep a descriptive frame of mind, not a judgemental one.
- Bullet the facts in short statements and in simple plain language (so that a child of ten can understand them).

- Try to be 100% objective.
- Get an expert or informed opinion.
- Test the veracity of all opinions and views. What assumptions are being made?
- Don't rely on one source for your information (e.g. your own organisation).
- When something appears out of kilter, assume first that it is a symptom of a deeper underlying problem.
- Don't stop simply because you believe you've found the problem. A complex problem is made of numerous inter-linking complications and causes – what makes you think you've discovered the whole iceberg?
- Keep reminding yourself that things are not always what they seem.
- Concentrate on the major issues relevant to the case. Don't get sidetracked analysing something that only has an indirect bearing on the subject. (See Pareto Analysis in Part 3).
- Apply the HW5 formula (how, what, why, when, where and who).

Summarise and circulate

When you feel that you have exhausted your scenario of all relevant facts, summarise the circumstances on no more than two or three pages – any longer than this might indicate overkill. Apply some of the techniques listed in Part 3 to help you map out the picture. If you are working with a group, circulate the summary of the circumstances so that everyone can agree on the facts. In my experience there are always those who will continue to disagree come hell or high water. But if they've had a chance to give their input and it is noted, their disagreement in subsequent sessions may be more muted!

I & G – Impediment and the Goal

It isn't that they can't see the solution. It's that they can't see the problem
– G K Chesterton

Let us consider the next two letters in CIGARS together as it's difficult to think of them independently. Were we to strictly deal with each letter as it appeared sequentially in GIGARS, we would find ourselves trying to define an impediment (or the main underlying problem) to a goal that we still had to define – a little like putting the cart before the horse! So, don't place too much emphasis on the actual letter *order* in CIGARS. The letters are meant more as reminders for each step in the problem-solving process rather than the order in which they should be carried out. Early on, whenever I'm tackling a problem, I try and keep a picture of the goal at the back of my mind, even while I'm still considering the circumstances. Although I often find that I have to revise this initial goal definition, by the time I'm focusing on the impediment (the problem), I have a pretty good idea of where I would like to end up.

It is good to keep considering your impediment and your goal in a fluid manner. Don't restrict your focus to either the goal or the impediment, but rather consider each simultaneously. This often results in a number of improving definitions for both your objective and the obstacle as your mind jockeys between the two. Don't be surprised if what you first regarded as an impediment turns out to be not a problem after all.

Take time to define

An accurate, succinct definition of the core problem is a major milestone. Problem solving starts with an accurate definition of the problem. But it would be mistake to assume that the definition of such occurs at the beginning of the whole problem-solving process. It is not unusual for a team to spend 70% of its time on a problem's definition with the other 30% being used to generate alternatives and identify a suitable solution. Working methodically through the circumstances of a problem scenario has the effect of sorting the wheat from the chaff. Issues are seen in context and suddenly one can perceive all the elements without unnecessary clutter. At times like this, it is hardly surprising that a tool as remarkable as the human mind is able to immediately identify numerous solutions. The fact is, as soon as we define the problem, our thinking around it quickly narrows. So don't get disheartened if the definition of the impediment seems to be taking most of the effort – more than likely, it will.

Keep the following in mind when you focus on the impediment and your goal:

- Most impediments have many underlying causes. Is the problem that you have identified simply a cause of something greater?
- Focus on your short-term goals. It's no good considering a goal that may only be achieved in the medium to long term.
- The impediment should have a relationship to your goal. If it is not linked then you haven't correctly identified it (or your wording of the goal is inappropriate).
- Although the identification of the impediment and the goal is largely a rational process, right-brain thinking can sometimes be useful in bringing new insights.
- Apply some of the techniques described in the next section (e.g. Fishbone Diagram, Affinity Diagram, Flowcharts, 5 Whys, etc) that aid in problem identity.
- Try defining the impediment in the words of someone who is outside your industry or business. How would somebody who does not have the same occupational baggage define the problem?
- Once the impediment has been defined, challenge others who are familiar with the situation to come up with a more succinct or accurate definition. If a better definition emerges adopt this and repeat the process.
- Restate your impediment and your goal in five different ways. This can lead to improvements.

It's important that everyone dealing with the problem (as well as those who will implement the solutions) is aware of the impediment and the goal. Write them down in simple plain language in as few words as possible – again, so that a child will understand them.

A – Alternatives

We cannot solve current problems with current thinking. Current problems are the result of current thinking. No problem can be solved from the same level of consciousness that created it.

– Albert Einstein

Let's now deal with the fourth letter in CIGARS. There are always a number of alternatives when determining how we will reach our goal. Even doing nothing is an alternative. In North East England (my birthplace), the Geordies have a saying that goes, 'When in doubt, do nought'. Hopefully our analysis will not leave us in doubt or with only the alternative of doing nothing to contemplate! In this stage of the exercise we are trying to develop as many alternative solutions (realistic and unrealistic) as possible. Just as the previous section was arguably more of a left-brain process than a right-brain one, the opposite applies here. Right-brain or divergent thinking will help you identify many more novel and original ideas than your logical brain can generate.

The more alternatives the better, so generate as many as you can. Don't concern yourself at this stage with implementation issues or possible side-effects. And just because your right brain is running amok is no reason for you to switch your left-brain off. A very good logical solution might be lurking undiscovered, so always try and use both types of thinking when you consider the alternatives. The only thing you must stop your analytical side from doing is being critical. Nothing kills off a creative line of thought better than derision.

Most of the alternatives that you identify will relate to the impediment – assuming of course that you have correctly identified this and that it is directly linked to your goal. But remember that the goal is the most important element. So if you can reach the goal by circumventing or bypassing the problem, all well and good. This is not always possible due to our definitions – the impediment is the one thing preventing us from reaching the goal (if there were other ways there might be no impediment) – but there are times when the application of lateral thought can discover something that was not previously perceived. The lesson: don't just limit your focus to the core problem itself – visualise your goal as well and think of possible novel ways in which it might be attained so that the problem is avoided or circumvented altogether. This is not a frequent occurrence, but at this stage of the problem-solving exercise it is sometimes possible to see short cuts that may resolve the situation. Don't allow this opportunity to pass by.

Not another brainstorm!

Most of you will be familiar with the brainstorming process. Although it's become a bit of a cliché and a panacea to most business ills, all too often it's carried out in a haphazard and ineffective manner. Those with strong or outgoing personalities tend to dominate proceedings, zany ideas are shot down before they can be properly noted or used as catalysts for further ideas and many intelligent participants choose to simply keep quiet. In every group there are those who love the sound of their own voices. If they haven't got anything to contribute to the issue under focus, they'll begin a train of thought quite unrelated to the subject under investigation. The result is that the meeting is railroaded to such an extent that it saps the motivation of the participants. This is unfortunate as brainstorming, if properly conducted, is an excellent way of generating alternatives for arriving at our goal. (See section 3 on how a brainstorming session should be handled).

Individuals or teams?

You may think that a group of people in a brainstorm is the best way of generating ideas. Actually, research studies have shown the opposite. Individuals working alone generate better ideas – both in number and in quality. Good teamwork can be difficult to achieve – if your staff members are not going to fully co-operate with one another, it might be more productive to manage them on an individual basis. A team of people would be wasteful if the problem was not a complex one or if it required a specific skill or technical expertise that a single individual could provide.

There's a lot to be said for teamwork in the problem-solving process. It creates a ventilation platform for those affected by the problem, and it can be useful in securing the commitment of the staff that will implement the solution. Complex problems often cover many different areas of the organisation and one or two individuals seldom offer the same knowledge and experience as those of a team. In addition, the consensus judgement of a group is in most cases more accurate than that of an individual, as is its analytical ability. Individuals working alone will probably come up with more and better ideas than they would have had they been in a group. But a group discussion is very effective in further discussing the initial ideas. This can lead to improvements on the original proposals and completely new ideas can also be unearthed in the process.

James Surowiecki, author of *The Wisdom of Crowds*, makes a number of relevant observations here. His view is that the very best decision-making body is a large diverse group of individuals. Even better than a skilled decision maker or expert! Alas, getting a large group of people to work on a project is impractical and you can't always draw on this collective wisdom. In the practical business world you will probably be faced with the choice between an individual or a small group. Surowiecki cautions his reader against the idiosyncrasies of the latter. It is possible for a small group to perform above the sum of its parts (i.e. smarter than the collective wisdom of its members), but this is not the rule. The group normally gets caught up in the dynamics of its own being (e.g. groupthink), resulting in poor decisions and unfortunate results. But that's no reason to abandon a group decision-making process – if you can get a small group (5–7 members from different disciplines) to gel without illusions of grandeur, it can be highly effective in the handling of problems. By the way, *The Wisdom of Crowds* is an excellent book, and I recommend it not just because it deals with group decision making, but also for its insights on problem solving in general.

Sensible and crazy

Usually the first alternatives identified when focusing on an impediment/goal tend to be the logical ones. Business is fundamentally based on left-brain thinking so it's not unusual for rationality to be first in raising its head. Some may have experience from similar situations in the past and the solutions applied then may be suggested again. Maybe other businesses with the same problem applied methods that proved effective and these are identified as possible alternatives. It's important not just to focus on the sensible and prudent solutions – try and come up with a few crazy and creative alternatives. When we develop alternatives we need to be totally non-critical. If people suspect that their wacko ideas may be sniggered at, they'll be reluctant to propose them. Remind everyone that the real village idiots are not the ones who suggest unusual ideas, but the empty vessels that deride them. Everyone should be made to feel that all ideas, whether rational or irrational, are welcomed as alternatives.

Creativity and new ideas

Innovation is one of the single biggest differentiating factors between outstanding companies and those of average performance. If a formula for creativity existed, it would have been bottled and marketed years ago. Coming up with creative ideas is a valuable skill in generating alternatives, but many people actually prevent themselves from doing this through their own thoughts of inadequacy. If you believe you will find a great idea, you will. If you think creative ideas escape you, then you're probably right.

It is a common belief that the older one gets, the less creative one becomes. Thus children are regarded as being more creative than adults. One of the reasons given is that adults with their greater experience base are more grounded in reality. Adults are also more risk averse and reluctant to propose something that might be regarded as ridiculous. Fortunately this does not mean that once you've reached adulthood, it's game over in terms of creativity. You simply have to reawaken the spirit of the child within you in order to improve your creative ability. But more on this later – there is a whole chapter on creativity at the end of Part 2.

R – Review

I have assumed that, in the exercise focusing on alternatives, you were able to contain any criticism you felt when new unusual ideas were suggested. You were expected to adopt predominantly right-brain thinking. But where divergent thinking was the driving force of the last exercise, the opposite applies to this section of the analysis. Under the alternatives section we have listed a number of ways of solving our problem. Not all of these will be practical, some will be impossible, others unaffordable, some ineffective, while a few may simply not suit the organisation (either the staff, or the powers that be). This is the point where we analyse the merits of each suggestion – in a constructive manner of course!

Every organisation is different and an alternative that appears fantastic in one company may be awkward in another. You need to identify the most novel and effective solutions according to criteria that are important to you or your group. For instance, if resources are relatively limited within your company, then cost may rank as an important criterion in the selection process. Another company may rate potential for revenue as a more important criterion than cost. Market share, shareholder interests, union issues, strategic positioning, customer relations, organisational change, time, are examples of other criteria. The point is that you have to evaluate the list of alternatives against the most important criteria for your business.

This needn't only be an organisational appraisal. If you were dealing with a personal problem, say a decision to move out of your present job, the criteria used for your evaluation might be future career prospects, salary implications, wife's career prospects or children's education (if relocation was involved) to mention just a few. The important thing is that you objectively assess each alternative according to relevant measures and not according to emotive issues.

Many of the alternatives from the last exercise may be similar or related. It may be possible to combine some of these into a composite solution that is superior to any of the individual elements. Look for such possible groupings before you start assessing each solution separately. Another good idea is to look at some of the alternatives that appear totally unrealistic, and to consider whether they can be reformulated in a way that falls within the boundaries of your parameters. For example, someone has proposed creating a TV advert as an alternative. The cost of the idea is way beyond the bounds of our marketing budget. But perhaps the prospect of co-operation with another company that regularly uses the medium of TV will make the idea feasible. Exploring this possibility further before disregarding the original idea could lead to a practical solution.

The review stage is more a rough filter than a final selection. You should aim at reducing your list of possibilities down to around three to five of the alternatives for the final analysis. You don't need to identify the optimal solution, just whittle the list of alternatives down to the best few. As I've pointed out, 'the best' needs to be gauged according to the values of the firm, the department, group or individual. If your company regards itself as being at the forefront of innovation, then a higher weighting will be given to those alternatives and ideas that are novel or may enhance the unique features of your product or service.

If economic considerations are paramount, a strong weighting may be given to criteria such as cost of implementation, productivity savings or organisational change.

A few points to remember:

- Explore the merits of each alternative thoroughly.
- Perform a rough factor analysis (i.e. try and group similar ideas into a composite solution or description).
- When assessing the alternatives get the views of others who were not part of the process in order to reduce the DEI.
- Giving a score to each alternative can help in ranking the solutions. For example each idea can be given a score from 1 to 5 for each of the criteria (e.g. cost, ease of implementation, impact, etc.) that are considered relevant.

- Focus on the key factors and avoid complexity (see Pareto Analysis and Occam's Razor in Part 3).
- Don't dismiss novel or original ideas – they are the seeds of innovation.
- If an original idea appears impractical, try and reformulate it in a way that will make it work.
- Aim at reducing the list of possible alternatives to around five.

S – Select

The great end of life is not knowledge but action

– Thomas Henry Huxley

Finally the last letter in CIGARS stands for select . You can have the best ideas or solutions in the world, but if a decision isn't taken regarding which to choose, then the exercise has been an unfortunate waste of time. At the end of the day somebody has to take action by deciding on a particular solution and more importantly, ensuring that it is correctly implemented.

If you've carried out the CIGARS procedure, you should have between three and five (you may have more) different alternative solutions to your impediment. These now have to be carefully considered and a final decision must be made. What typically happens in the review process is that one gets a good appreciation of which alternative is the best. But even the best idea is no better than the very worst if it remains an object for contemplation and reflection. You have to move the solution from theory to practice. You have to decide which solution(s) is (are) best and you need to take action.

Up to now I have tended to speak of the one optimal solution. This is misleading because in reality many solutions can be applied simultaneously to solve or negate the problem. In Part 3 you will find the useful problem-solving technique called Force Field Analysis. This method recognises and applies numerous solutions to a particular problem or issue. Also, if you have been dealing with a complex problem, you'll realise that it has many facets and consequently an array of interrelated solutions.

But to make things simpler here, let's assume that we are looking for one definitive solution. We have managed to reduce our list down to seven alternatives, which we've labelled A, B, C, D, E, F & G. How do we decide which of these will be best? Unfortunately there's not a universal checklist or screening device. Much will depend on your particular situation and your values. A consensus view from a group discussion can be accurate and effective, though there may be other issues at play of which the members are unaware. But as a general rule the consensus judgement of a group should be valued above that of an individual.

Pair Ranking

One useful method for selecting items is *pair ranking*. I've chosen to include it here (rather than in Part 3) because it is one of the most effective methods in selection. If it was mentioned merely as one of many techniques described later, you might not take the time to understand and apply it. It is one the best techniques you'll learn from this book and I urge you to take the time to do so. Pair ranking recognises that humans have difficulty choosing between many items, but are fairly clear minded when it comes to choosing between two options. Consider our first two alternatives A and B. Which is superior? Let's assume we pick B. Make a mark against B. Now repeat the exercise between A and C. Which is superior? Now we feel A is better. So make a mark against A. Repeat the procedure for A and D, A and E and A and F. Now move to B – we've already scored A and B, so we can start here with B and C. Once you've pair ranked B with the rest, do the same for C, D, E , F and G (actually G will have been gauged once you've finished with F!). Count the number of marks against each – the one with the maximum marks is best.

It's more efficient to carry out the analysis on a matrix. An example of this is given below. I have used the same seven alternatives A to G and I have purposely blocked off the one side of the matrix (by placing Xs in each box) since it is redundant. Moving down the first column, I first consider A versus B (I think B is best, so I put a B in this block) then A versus C (now an A in this block). Once you finished with the first column move onto the next and carry on until the matrix is filled. Each time you are only considering two factors and selecting the one that you feel is better. At the end of the exercise count the letters in the matrix to see which one is listed most often.

Matrix for pair ranking seven alternatives

	A	**B**	**C**	**D**	**E**	**F**	**G**
A	X	X	X	X	X	X	X
B	B	X	X	X	X	X	X
C	A	B	X	X	X	X	X
D	A	B	D	X	X	X	X
E	E	E	E	E	X	X	X
F	A	B	C	D	E	X	X
G	G	G	G	G	E	G	X

Count the letters in the matrix: A = 3, B = 4, C = 1, D = 2, E = 6, F = 0, G = 5. E is therefore the best alternative. If you've been consistent throughout, each alternative should have a different score, making the ranking easy. But we're not always 100% logical and consistent and very often a few of the items get identical scores. In such cases you will need to make a final call to decide which is superior (this tends to happen when you are pair ranking many variables).

You can take this analysis one step further by repeating the procedure for different criteria. Each of your alternatives will have different features and these features will mean different things to different people. You may wish to assess your alternatives in terms of these different criteria since it is difficult to determine which is 'best' unless you have a thorough frame of reference. If you reflect upon the exercise above, you might find that what you subjectively considered to the best in each case was in fact the cheaper of the two options. In other words, subconsciously you used cost as your overriding criterion. But now you recognise that while each alternative may have a different cost implication, each will also have a different impact in the short term and some are easier to implement than others. Since these are also important considerations in making a selection, you need to repeat the whole pair ranking exercise for each different criterion. You would start by asking: In terms of cost, which is better, A or B, A or C, ..., F or G? Total the scores. Now perform the same exercise, but the question becomes: In terms of implementation, which is better, A or B, etc. etc? You have chosen to select three criteria here, so you naturally end up with three sets of pair-ranked scores. How do you now decide which alternative is best?

You begin by assigning a weighting (between 0 and 1) to each of the criteria (the sum of the weightings must equal one). If you had four criteria and you felt they were equally important, you would assign a weighting of 0.25 to each. But it is more common for one or two of the measures to be seen as more important than the others. In our example we have pair ranked the seven alternatives according to cost, ease of implementation and short-term impact. These scores are reflected in the table below (I haven't included the matrices where we pair ranked the alternatives according to implementation and impact, but I assume you have followed the drift). Suppose we feel that the short-term impact of the solution chosen should be the most important consideration and that the other two, cost and ease of implementation, are secondary details. Consequently, we have decided to give the weightings of 0.1, 0.3 and 0.6 to cost, implementation and impact respectively.

Pair rankings according to different criteria

Alternative	Cost	Implementation	Impact
A	3	6	0
B	4	0	2
C	1	5	4
D	2	2	5
E	6	3	1
F	0	4	6
G	5	1	3

We now multiply each pair-ranked score with the respective weighting and sum these across for each alternative:

	Cost (0.1)	Implem. (0.3)	Impact (0.6)	Sum	Rank
A	3 x 0.1 = 0.3	6 x 0.3 = 1.8	0 x 0.6 = 0	2.1	5
B	4 x 0.1 = 0.4	0 x 0.3 = 0	2 x 0.6 = 1.2	1.6	7
C	1 x 0.1 = 0.1	5 x 0.3 = 1.5	4 x 0.6 = 2.4	4.0	2
D	2 x 0.1 = 0.2	2 x 0.3 = 0.6	5 x 0.6 = 3.0	3.8	3
E	6 x 0.1 = 0.6	3 x 0.3 = 0.9	1 x 0.6 = 0.6	2.1	5
F	0 x 0.1 = 0	4 x 0.3 = 1.2	6 x 0.6 = 3.6	4.8	1
G	5 x 0.1 = 0.5	1 x 0.3 = 0.3	3 x 0.6 = 1.8	2.6	4

Now alternative F appears to be best. If we had relied upon our first pair ranking score, when we realised that we had rated the alternatives on cost alone, we might have chosen E (where F got a score of zero!). As you can see, by taking into account other considerations and weighting these according to their perceived importance, a much more accurate picture can be achieved.

Pair ranking with weighted criteria is a very effective (albeit laborious) method of selecting the best alternative. Obviously the type and number of criteria are something you and your colleagues need to agree upon, as are the values (or weightings) which you accord to each. It's often surprising how different the end analysis turns out from the initial selection when no pair ranking was performed. Try it for yourself on a list of things that you want to rank. How about seeing which new car you should buy? Your criteria might be any of fuel economy, safety, acceleration, resale value, top speed, comfort and space, reliability, image, price, service costs, etc. If you have a long list of criteria, you may need to reduce it to a more manageable few. Simply perform a pair ranking on the criteria themselves. So, in the car example, you would ask yourself: Which is more important to me; fuel economy or safety, fuel economy or acceleration? and so on. At the end of the exercise you'll have a score for each and you can identify the top three or four criteria for your decision. Remember to weight them according to your preferences and check that the weights all total to one!

A more useful application might be assessing competing proposals that your company has received from a tender – the criteria here could be cost, guarantee, company reputation, disruption factors, etc. Again, whichever criteria you select, you'll need to weight them according to the values of your company. Another perennial favourite is the decision on where to hold the next company function. These decisions are always laced with emotion. With weighted ranking you can get everyone to agree on the basis of the decision and how it will be carried out. Some people may not like the final outcome, but no one will be able to question the way in which the outcome was derived.

The applications for weighted pair ranking are innumerable and I recommend that you start practising this technique whenever you have the opportunity, because it is only with practice that you will become proficient. Once mastered, it will become a tool for life!

At the end of the day when you've made your selection, perform a reality check. Will the selected alternative prove impractical? Perhaps some related issues have been overlooked? It's not uncommon for someone, or a team of people, to be so wrapped up in a problem that they simply don't see what outsiders consider blatantly obvious. It might be good to get the opinions of people who have not been a part of the process but are still qualified to give a valued opinion. Learn to recognise the sound of your intuitive voice as well. In the tragedy *Hamlet*, Polonius advises his son Laertes: 'to thine own self be true'. Some believe that Shakespeare borrowed this line from the Socratic maxim, 'Know thyself'. Whatever the background, they are both examples of profound wisdom in elegant brevity.

Changes occur with implementation, not with planning

An idea that is developed and put into action is more important than an idea that exists only as an idea
> – **Prince Gautama Siddhartha (Buddha)**

This world belongs to those that do, not to those that think. Don't for one minute believe that just because you've managed to discover a suitable solution your situation is rectified. Finding the solution is only the halfway point – not literally of course, but if you slip up in your implementation, it might just as well be. Once you've arrived at a suitable solution, you have to ensure that it is put into action. You need to plan the implementation and then trigger the process that will bring it all about. In my experience, businesses that fail to achieve their potential do so, not because they don't have a strategy or plan, but rather because the plan was poorly implemented.

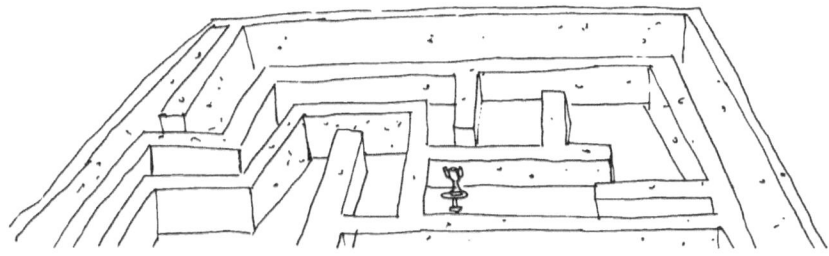

Once you have your solution sit back and take a helicopter perspective of your situation. Where are you now? Where do you ultimately want to be? Imagine yourself at your desired destination. Now think – just prior to reaching this, what had to be in place before we made the final jump to our goal? Again, in order to reach this point, what were the platforms that allowed us to reach the penultimate stage? Keep working in this manner until you have successfully identified all the inter-linking stepping-stones between your present state and your future goal. Sometimes this can be quite a complicated procedure, and it's a good idea to carry out this exercise with a group of people who are all capable of making constructive inputs. In this way you will minimise the risk of overlooking an important stage.

When you have mapped out the implementation in terms of stages you should try and put time estimates to the various sub-tasks. If your team is making these estimates and the same members are going to be responsible for implementation, your estimates will probably be excessively conservative. People tend to overestimate the time they require for a particular task. And according to Parkinson's Law, if ten days are allocated for a particular job, it will only be completed in that time, not before. The late Mark McCormack, founder of the IMG sports empire, suggested putting Parkinson's Law into reverse. Since work expands to fill the time allocated for its completion, he suggested that work similarly contracts to fill a shrinking amount of time for its completion. As McCormack put it, if your most important customer requests something within ten days, agree to do it in five. More often than not, you'll be able to achieve this. As an avid rugby fan, I must have watched hundreds of live broadcasts of the sport. I'm always amazed at how many times a match is turned around in the final couple of minutes of injury time. I suppose that, when time is tight, the team only then adopts a focus and commitment that hitherto had escaped it. That's Parkinson's Law in reverse for you – a very good rule of thumb to keep at the back of your mind.

The next important phase of the implementation is allocation of responsibility. Don't make the mistake of giving a committee or group of people joint responsibility for actions or deadlines. The chances are good that the deadline will be missed, or the work will have been carried out in a half-hearted manner and no one will accept responsibility and make amends. You're better off identifying the individuals within your company upon whom you can depend. Split the work amongst this group of reliable people but make sure that each has a specific responsibility. These needn't be people with authority (many a bright young spark with no authority is only too willing to prove his or her worth) but they need to understand what is expected of them in terms of the deliverables and the timing.

Once the implementation has been agreed and the work has been allocated, your next focus is control. Just as coming up with a solution doesn't solve the problem, so planning the implementation doesn't ensure action unless you introduce control. Regular feedback sessions should be held and you have to constantly monitor progress against objectives. Naturally delays will occur (Murphy's Law!), but picking them up as early as possible, allows for corrective action to be taken. These progress meetings need not be lengthy affairs, just short snappy status reports where the implications of the various delays or gains can be factored into the project.

As I've mentioned, there will be times when you hit a crisis. If so, my advice is that you look for solutions long before you look for culprits.

Assuming your implementation has gone more or less according to plan, the question that now remains is whether the problem still exists. In the real world we can't simply assume that it has vanished or that it has been resolved. For all we know, the situation might have been aggravated by our implementation – although this is not very likely. Nevertheless, once you are satisfied with the implementation of your solution(s), you should investigate your circumstances to check that the problem has been dealt with. Your solution may have spawned a number of new, albeit smaller, problems. If so, you will need to identify and resolve these before they grow in complexity. As with most of the processes described in this book, try and get the inputs of many in this post-analysis rather than the views of an interested few.

Remember the following:

- When you are assessing your final few alternatives make sure that everyone is clear on the underlying criteria for the choice.
- Avoid making emotional decisions.
- Paired ranking with weighted criteria is an effective method of determining the relative value of different alternatives or elements.
- If two alternatives look equally suitable, go for the one that you intuitively feel is better.
- Perform a last-minute reality check after you've made a decision.
- Don't think that the problem is solved once the solution is agreed. Many excellent solutions have fallen by the wayside due to poor implementation. Spend time planning every element and phase of the solution's execution.
- Keep deadlines tight. Apply Parkinson's Law in reverse.
- Identify dependable individuals and assign responsibility for the various milestones. Don't make committees or groups responsible for key tasks.
- Monitor the progress and measure the results.

Well, there you have it. CIGARS may not give you the solution you seek, but in most cases it will give you the best chance of finding one. As I mentioned earlier, once you've applied it a couple of times and seen how effective it is in structuring your thoughts, you'll always remember to use it. Don't criticise or disregard its basic approach on the grounds of it being rudimentary and simplistic. Actually, in my experience, the simplest things are very often the most difficult to accomplish. I know many intelligent and highly educated people who would be a lot better off today had they followed the CIGARS analysis before they arrived at certain decisions on various challenges they faced in the past. Don't be one of them.

Rediscovering your creative ability

An idea is a feat of association — Robert Frost

Since most of us have lost the creativity of our younger years, I thought the title of this chapter was fitting. Imagine your brain as a creative nuclear power station. As you progressed towards adulthood, life has successively inserted carbon rods into the reactor core to the point where you feel as if your creative ability has dwindled. That's the bad news. The good news is that you can reverse the process. By the end of this chapter you'll be well-equipped to remove the rods and reawaken the fires of old. In short, you'll start a chain reaction that will allow your brain to perform its highest purpose – to develop new ideas.

Creativity is the most important skill in problem solving. While it's possible to solve many problems without being overly creative, the addition of it will always give you an edge. There are many excellent books on creativity available today and anyone wishing to improve their creative abilities is advised to visit their local bookstore, library or better still search and buy online. I cannot hope, in a single chapter, to fully cover the subject. But I can give you a few useful guidelines that will help you generate better ideas in the future. It might be a mere scratch on the surface, but I hope it will lead to an itch that you'll never satisfy.

Ad agencies (and similar marketing companies) pride themselves on the creative ability of their staff. I suppose it's to be expected, with creativity being their most marketable commodity. But if someone told me that the creative potential of the staff in an ad agency and that of the staff in a government department were roughly the same, I wouldn't be that surprised. We're all blessed with heaps of creative ability and it's normal for it to be equally distributed. Mind you, we're talking about potential here; not actual creativity itself or the number of new ideas generated over a period of time. If the latter is to be the measure, I'm sure the ad agency would win hands down. The reason is that ad agencies understand the working conditions that encourage and stimulate creative thinking amongst their staff. And generally they create those conditions much better than most government departments do. It's sad to realise that much of the creative resources of bureaucratic organisations is frittered away as a result of rigid systems and procedures that demand compliance and conformity.

Many people believe they are not creative or imaginative. So long as they believe this they are 100% correct. This paralysing effect from our thoughts is not limited to creativity. Years ago I lectured a course in mathematics to postgraduate students. Many of the students feared they were going to fail the course because they didn't have mathematical minds. Fortunately I was able to convince them that all of us have minds capable of very complex mathematical calculations even though we may believe the opposite. Once their confidence in their own abilities improved, no one had a problem in passing the course. The same applies to creativity. The first step in becoming more creative is an inner belief that you will be able to come up with new and innovative ideas. Belief in one's ability to accomplish a task is the most powerful force for success – and vice versa; belief in one's inability is the most debilitating force. The choice is yours as to which path you'll take.

Recognise your undeniable creative talent and remain convinced that in any situation you'll be able to find a new idea.

Ideas are infinite

The more you think about it, the more self-evident this concept becomes. After all, if ideas were finite, we would often experience instances where we exhaust all the possible variations on a particular issue. You might feel this way at times but then suddenly someone comes up with something that, once revealed is so obvious you want to kick yourself for not thinking of it. You see, when you think about it, you begin to realise that there's probably no end to the number of different ideas that can be developed around an item or a concept. James Web Young, a noted US copywriter in the 20th century, defined an idea quite simply *as a new combination of old elements.* And to give you an impression of just how many ways old elements can be combined in new ways, imagine having a small container of coloured glitter. Now pour it onto a flat white surface – say a large piece of paper. Think how many different patterns you could make on the paper by spreading the glitter around. Well that's about how many new combinations one can create out of old elements. If you want further proof consider music. We've had an innumerable number of different songs and pieces of music in the past and an even greater number awaits us in the future. There is no end to the number of new combinations that can be made from the elements of music.

One problem we seem to have is that, in reality, we act as if ideas were finite. We subconsciously believe that the best ideas on a particular subject have already been discovered or taken by someone else. We feel it's not worth our while to try and consider a few remaining modifications that would probably have been discovered before now anyway if they were good ideas. Can you see how such thinking hobbles any effort to consider an improvement or innovation? Can you also see how this thinking would only make sense if the set of ideas were finite? It might also be helpful to remember these words from the American poet Maya Angelou: *You cannot use up creativity. The more you use the more you have.* You're not swimming in a finite pool.

There is always a new idea waiting to be discovered – on everything.

Laugh and have fun

I've always believed that a sense of humour is one of the most important attributes to have in business – whether you're a manager or not. The ability to laugh at most things (including yourself) will allow you to remain sane in a world gone mad. It will also make you more interesting to your colleagues and will energise your creative spirit. Again, ad agencies are cases in point. The directors go to lengths to ensure that they are fun places to work in because a fun environment is a good breeding ground for new ideas. This reminds me of the times when I used to entertain my colleagues at work by adding captions to various photos cut from newspapers or magazines. Many of the captions took playful swipes either at the way we were doing business or at some of the more colourful individuals who worked there. Each day I'd create a new picture and staff members made a point of dropping by my office to see the latest contribution. It was a fun time in my life. Coincidentally it was also a period in which my creative skills were at a high. I seemed able to come up with new solutions to problems or raise new suggestions for how we could do things. I'm convinced that the fun I had at work over this time contributed positively to my creative ability.

Serious people struggle to find new ideas. If you can't lighten up, postpone your creative session until you can.

Break the mould

All of us are creatures of habit. We eat the same breakfast each morning, we comb our hair the same way, we drive to work along the same route, we read the same newspapers, we watch the same TV channels, we prefer sitting in the same seat – there's no end to the amount of regularity we embrace in our daily lives. And if for any reason this routine is broken, we feel irritated and unsettled. Being in one's comfort zone with all its familiarities is a secure feeling. It's not, however, the best environment for new inputs. In your quest for new ideas, in order to increase your chances of success, you should preferably be experiencing a life with many changes, not one characterised by routine.

Most of us resist change, especially if others are imposing those changes. But if you intentionally introduce change as a means of experiencing new perspectives, the disruption is entirely acceptable, even exciting. And that's what I suggest you do. Embrace change wherever and whenever you can. Read a magazine or journal that you wouldn't ordinarily read. Listen to a radio station that you've never listened to before. Talk to people at work that up until now have been relative strangers – listen to them with an interest that encourages them to open up to you. When surfing the net, avoid your usual sites. Use a search engine to explore fields that you think might give you a few interesting angles or alternatives. If you rely on the TV for your daily news, buy a newspaper instead. Read different newspapers on different days. If you struggle to get up in the mornings, get up even earlier and go for a run/walk before breakfast. I could on until the cows come home! The trick is to turn this exercise into a continual game. Try and be aware of your daily habits. Once you recognise them, derive a playful satisfaction in adopting the role of a maverick to your established persona. Not only will you prime yourself for new ideas, you could just make your life that little bit more interesting.

Identify your daily habits and purposely strive to do things differently.

Change your perspective

The easiest thing in the world is to consider something from one's own point of view. But you will gain so much more if you consider it from another's – especially if that other person is someone who is directly affected by the matter under question. The objective here is not to reach a position where you understand or appreciate where the other person is coming from. You are not trying to win points for empathy here. You are rather trying to vigorously explore the situation as if you were that other person seeking a new alternative. So much conflict and deadlock is due to people being too thick-skinned to consider a situation from a perspective other than their own. Not only does this lead to an impasse, it also severely limits their ability to generate new ideas.

Look at things from different points of view.

An ever-expanding warehouse

On his Ziggy Stardust album (still one of my favourites!), David Bowie referred to his brain as a warehouse with no room to spare. It may be a colourful description, but it's a false one – your brain has so much room to spare, it's unlikely that you'll ever fill it. And even though you may think that information stored years ago and subsequently forgotten is lost, indications are that your subconscious mind still has access to it. Perhaps this is why we sometimes can't explain how, or where, or why we got a particular idea. We subconsciously combined old elements (forgotten by our conscious minds) in new way.

If we have this unlimited storage capacity for old elements and if ideas are new combinations of these, it follows that you should never stop seeking out new information and concepts. And don't believe that because you're an engineer, your pursuit of knowledge should be focused on publications such as *Popular Mechanics* and the like. You need to draw upon as diverse a range of resources as possible if you want to come up with interesting ideas. Most of us specialise in terms of a career and, for a certain period, we need to focus our studies in order to qualify. But once this is over, you should develop an active interest in many unrelated fields – that is, if you want to become good at discovering new ideas. So if you're an accountant, in addition to keeping abreast of developments in this field (and others that you personally find interesting), you could read up on environmental issues, agriculture, science, poetry, history, religions, world orchestras, foreign languages and customs and many, many more. There's probably a direct relationship between the variety of subjects stored in your mind and the number of interesting ideas that you're able to come up with.

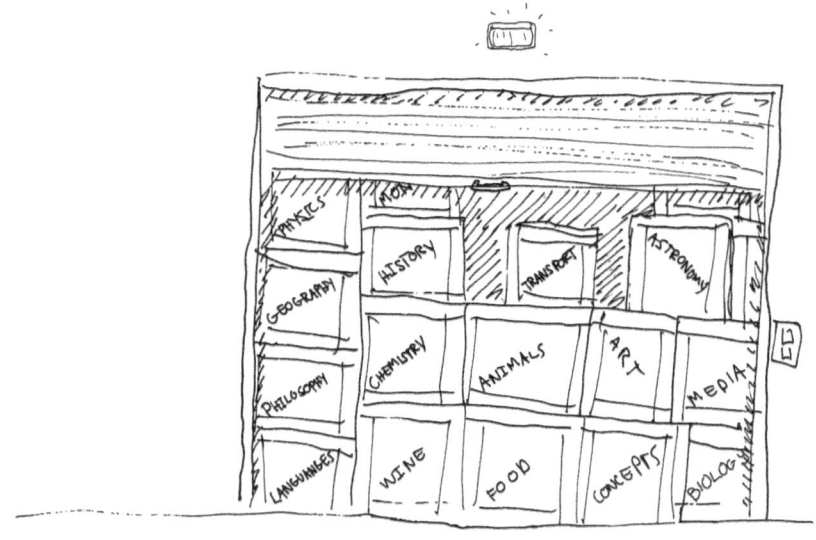

Your brain is an infinite warehouse – if you want to improve your idea-generating ability you need to keep storing goods of an ever-increasing variety.

Become a child

Numerous studies show that the level of creativity within children far exceeds that of adults. One's creative ability deteriorates with age, so that by the time you reach 40, a child in nursery school is likely to be more than five times your superior when it comes to creativity. This is a generalisation of course, but one that can't be denied. Children are better than adults when it comes to creative thinking. Why is this?

Firstly, adults are more inhibited than children. They are more conscious of their surroundings and what other people may think of them. This tends to confine their inclination to speak spontaneously when thinking of new ideas. Secondly, adults are more aware of the realities of life – their enthusiasm for new projects or ideas has been diluted through past failure. It might also be due to adults favouring left-brain thinking and analysis over a right-brain perspective. These are just a few of the reasons and we needn't think of others here. The good news is that you can redevelop the creative ability of your youth simply by the way you think.

When seeking a creative solution, imagine what sort of questions a child of five would ask. Would they be worried about persistently asking the same question if they felt the answer was inadequate? Of course not! Do likewise. Be courageous in what you think and say. Use both sides of your brain when thinking about a situation or problem. Appreciate the simple things that children enjoy. Become as active as a child. Take an interest in everything. Delight in making unusual and original associations. Lose the distorted perception that years of adulthood have created. Creativity is more within the domain of the mischievous child than it is within that of the responsible adult.

Imagine yourself as a child with boundless energy, infectious enthusiasm and an insatiable appetite for knowledge. Become that person.

Take an interest in art
Some believe you can divide people into two categories, those that appreciate the arts, and those that do not. This is a specious claim. I believe we all value the beauty contained in various art forms – it's what distinguishes us as human beings. It may be that one's past background or environment has not been conducive to developing this interest, but this is hardly a reason to state that one has no capacity for discernment or appreciation of various art forms.

Most of the world's greatest inventors and scientists had, or have, strong links to art. Ask each person in a group to list the five most creative people they know (point out that it can be anyone from the past or present). You'll find that most of the people mentioned will be artists. No surprise here since we tend to associate creativity with art. Artists by their nature are creative. The fact that many people don't consider themselves artistic is one of the reasons why they believe they are not particularly creative. If you are one of those people, you will be amazed at the latent artistic talents within you. Simply enrol in an art class (it can be in painting, drawing, writing, music, acting, whatever) – I guarantee you will discover qualities and skills that you never dreamed you possessed.

Make an effort to visit the theatre. Read the classics. If you choose to visit an art museum, read up on the artists and their lives – study the works and understand what it was they wished to convey. Keep a sketchbook and draw images of thoughts you have from time to time. Learn to appreciate many different types of music – see each as an expression of someone else's creativity. If possible, learn to play a musical instrument. Walk round a music shop and pick an instrument that looks interesting to you. Sing whenever you feel like it. Learn how to dance. You have nothing to lose and so much to gain.

Develop a positive attitude towards all art forms – don't be surprised when the artist within you is unleashed.

Ninety-nine per cent perspiration

The proportion of effort, in the words of Thomas Edison, required before reaching a level of genius. The other one per cent is inspiration. Given the brilliance and scope of his inventions, Edison would be one of the most qualified people to pass an opinion on the subject. So if you thought that creativity is all about relaxing in an idyllic setting, contemplating new concepts over a bottle of cabernet, you are sadly mistaken. Creativity involves a lot of hard work.

We have all experienced the sudden flash of a new idea. Maybe it was while we were trying to fall asleep or perhaps while lying in the bath. The time it took for our minds to consider the idea was probably very short – virtually instantaneous. I suppose that is the one per cent to which Edison referred. We make the mistake of perceiving that flash of brilliance as creativity itself when in fact it is only a small fraction of the whole process. In order for your subconscious mind to reach a new and original solution you had to seed it with data relevant to your situation. Ideas don't just form out of nothing. They need to develop like crystals around a framework of knowledge and information. Each stage in the process – gathering information, analysing it, considering it from different perspectives, thinking of different associations and combinations, investigating connections to other things, reconsidering your impediment and your goal – is just as important as the next in the creative cycle. There are no short cuts. It's a hard slog, but a very rewarding one.

Be prepared for hard work if you're looking for original and constructive ideas.

Associate and combine

The first barometer was created when Evangelista Torricelli combined the properties of mercury with those of atmospheric pressure. Richard Trevithick combined the steam engine with the horse-drawn transport systems used in coalmines to invent the first train. By observing a children's pastime, Barnes Wallis devised a bomb that bounced on water. Most inventions and discoveries were merely new combinations of things that were known before. And many of the best ideas came from associations drawn from very diverse fields. If you want to come up with new ideas start developing your ability to associate and combine things.

There are many association games that one can play where the similarities and the differences between two unrelated items or concepts are identified and discussed. Notice I say two unrelated items. It is very easy to compare two related items such as a knife and a fork or a cow and a glass of milk. But your chances of coming up with anything original are not very good if you do this. Rather, the next time you are looking for ideas relating to a particular issue, pick a random word and think of all the attributes that can be linked between that word and your problem. And when I say random, I mean random. Don't page through the dictionary until you see a word that appeals to you. Decide upon a referencing system beforehand, pick a random number and look to see what word corresponds to that number in a dictionary according to your system. Alternatively you can pick one of the words that I have listed in Association Words on page in Part 3 of this book. Once you have picked a word (randomly), write down as many attributes or characteristics of that word as you can think of. Persevere with the word you have selected – don't simply pick another word which you feel is easier to 'dissect'. After you've done this, think of the similarities between your listed features and those of your problem issue. Don't worry if some of your associations seem weird or bizarre – bear in mind that you are always trying to seek out the unconventional.

Leonardo da Vinci said that in some way, everything is connected to everything else. The practice of association allows you to put this principle into practice. Start making associations between diverse things and you will soon discover what Leonardo meant. There is always a link from one thing to every other thing. Once you realise this you will become an active observer of the world around you. May you never tire of seeking unusual ties between unrelated objects and concepts.

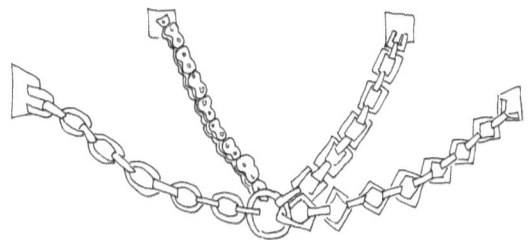

Develop your ability to identify the key features of things and concepts and practice linking these to other things in the universe.

Rules, what rules?

Consider the parameters and rules that we associate with things – how can these be twisted or bent to suit the situation? Why not consider breaking them? I'm not suggesting that you become an anarchist, but sometimes it's useful to assume that there are no rules and that anything is possible. A fictional example of this is found in the excellent 1999 movie, *The Matrix*, from Warner Bros. In one scene, Morpheus (Laurence Fishburne) encourages Neo (Keanu Reeves) to free his mind by regarding reality as a simple construct of his perception. He points out that some of the rules governing this reality can be bent while others can be broken – it is up to Neo to fashion it as he pleases. We may not be able to mould our world as successfully as Neo did, but we are certainly free to consider and suggest every possibility capable of being imagined.

Not letting rules shackle your thoughts isn't easy to achieve. So many of the rules that we live by are virtually hard-wired in our brains. We often don't think of something because we subconsciously disregarded that avenue as a cul-de-sac. But consider this: if you are going to discover something original, if you are going to break into new territory, you might have to go where some people say you can't. You need to be bold enough to think of something that, up until now, others didn't think of considering because they believed it wasn't within the rules.

Don't let rules inhibit your quest for an original idea.

Make a start

If I were restricted to giving one single piece of advice to you for generating ideas, then I think it would be this. The best way of coming up with many ideas is to have one in the first place. I know this sounds illogical, but what I'm trying to show is how important it is to begin the process. One idea leads to another. Even if the first one is a bad one, it is still an idea. It will act as a trigger for another one, which in turn will lead to another and so on. In your quest for brilliant ideas, think of every idea as a stepping-stone across a turbulent river. You have to use a few smaller shaky stones in order to reach the larger stable ones where you feel more comfortable.

Some people are afraid of proposing ideas because they fear criticism. If you have a group of people, begin by pointing out that all criticism is unwelcome. Maybe you can have a fining system – each criticism incurs a monetary fine. Once everyone feels at ease to speak his or her mind, drop a snowball and see how it gathers momentum. You will also get to realise another interesting feature when it comes to ideas. The more ideas you come up with, the better the quality of those ideas.

You will only struggle to find ideas if you are afraid to make a start. Begin with something, anything, and allow your mind to freewheel.

Incubation

Take a break or, better still, start working on something else. One very good method for coming up with a novel solution to a problem is to actually forget about it. After a period of intense concentration on the situation (i.e. the circumstances, the issue and the goal), put the whole affair on the back burner and remove it completely from your mind. Don't even make a mental note of when you next plan to revisit the subject. Switch off any anxiety that you may have felt as a result of not finding a solution and leave the matter to a higher power – your subconscious. This has the effect of putting the problem into incubation. Now you may think that nothing will happen until you reopen the case, but you'd be wrong. A little while thereafter (it could be hours or even days) a unique and novel solution will spring to your mind out of the blue. I don't know why or how this works, but it does.

Whenever she lost something, my Mum would say a silent prayer to Saint Anthony asking for his help in finding the lost item. She would then stop her search and forget about the loss, since she believed with absolute conviction that Saint Anthony would find it for her. And more times than not, he did! Now I'm not sure if a patron saint of creativity or problem solving exists, but I see similarities between this method of putting a problem to rest and my Mum's practice whenever she mislaid an item. I suppose her faith in Saint Anthony's ability to uncover things was similar to the trust you need to have in the power of your subconscious to deliver a solution.

If you reach a dead end and you are struggling to find a new idea, drop everything and concentrate on something else. Let your subconscious take over.

Record your thoughts
Each day we go about our work, we meet various people, we read interesting pieces of information, we experience different sensations – and most of it unfortunately passes us by. We may store these experiences in our subconscious, but we lose the keys to all the storage bins. If we had a quick referencing system to all the information that was housed in our brains, perhaps ideas wouldn't be so elusive.

If you're serious about improving your creative ability, then do the following. Visit a quality bookstore and purchase one of those hard-cover journals where all the pages are blank (or lined if you prefer). If you can't find it in a bookstore, try a bookbinding firm. You could of course use a plain exercise book (as used in schools), but these aren't as substantial as the hard-covered ones – and you want a bit of gravitas!

This book is now going to become your ideas journal. Every interesting thought you have, everything interesting thing you see, every interesting person you meet, every interesting place you visit, everything interesting thing you read, in fact every new thing that comes into your life, make a note of it in your journal. How did you feel at the time you experienced it? What did it make you think of? What possible links could there be from this to other things? Get into the habit of recording your experiences and your new ideas. Each person's approach is different and best for them. If you can, try and record your experiences and thoughts with diagrams and illustrations. They are so much more effective than words. And please don't think that you are not sufficiently talented to draw. This is your journal, your diagrams, your interpretations – it's not something that is about to be published for all to see.

Keeping an ideas journal is hard work – that's why I asked whether you were serious about becoming more creative. Nowadays very few people still use paper to record their thoughts. Many of us choose to record things on computers, PDAs or even cell phones. However, recording the significant happenings of your life in electronic format just doesn't hack it. By all means use your portable electronic device to note things when they happen. Or jot them down in a small notebook that you can keep handy in your pocket or bag. But make it part of your daily routine to transfer these thoughts and experiences to your journal (replete with diagrams if possible). How often should you do this? Well, how often is your life slightly different from what it has been before? Exactly! Try and keep your journal updated as much as you can. Once you reach the end of the book, begin a new one.

This is not just about recording ideas and maintaining impressive journals as keepsakes for your grandchildren. One of the main reasons for wanting to record your thoughts and ideas is that they would probably be forgotten if you didn't write them down. The same will happen if you bury your journal away in some bookcase once it is complete. Your journal needs to become a working document – something to which you refer on a periodic basis, especially at times when you are looking for new ideas. Reading it will be nourishment for your mind.

Keep a personal journal of all the new thoughts, ideas and experiences that occur in your life. Read through it on a regular basis.

I thought it might be appropriate to conclude this chapter on creativity with a quote from a leading creative mind, Albert Einstein, who said:

Imagination is more important than knowledge, for imagination is limitless.

Part 3

Useful Problem-solving Techniques

It requires a very unusual mind to make an analysis of the obvious
– Alfred North Whitehead

As I mentioned earlier, CIGARS is a mechanism for structuring a business problem (or any problem for that matter). I can't guarantee that you will find a solution, but it's my view that if you apply it, you will give yourself the best chance of doing so. Since CIGARS is not a universal problem solver, I have decided, in this part of the book, to include descriptions of a few popular problem-solving techniques. These are only brief summaries which in most cases hardly do justice to the techniques themselves. But I believe they are sufficient for you to comprehend the technique and to start applying it in practice. You may struggle at first, but I assure you, the more you try them, the better you will get at using them. Some will appeal to you more than others, and some are limited in terms of their application to the circumstances of the situation. But I encourage you to become familiar with many of them and to start using them selectively in addressing the problems within your business. In most cases I've presented the techniques in a standard format (What, Why, When, Who and How) to help in identifying the appropriate technique at the different stages in the problem solving cycle.

I have purposely chosen to not to provide numerous examples or case studies here. I've found that people in business usually want the pith of something rather than the orchard in which it grew. A short guide on how to implement something is, in my opinion, more valuable than a history of cases illustrating how a few people fared in their problem-solving endeavours. I trust you share my view.

List of Techniques

- Affinity Diagrams
- Association Words
- Brainstorming
- Comic Relief
- Decision Trees
- Fishbone Diagram
- Five Whys
- Flowcharts
- Force Field Analysis

- Lateral Thinking
- Lotus Blossom Technique
- Matrix Diagram
- Mind Maps
- Nominal Group Technique
- Problem Definition
- Pros, Cons and Fixes
- Reversing the Problem
- Rival Hypotheses
- Useful Theories and Principles
- Weighted Ranking

Affinity Diagrams

What?

- A group technique where new ideas pertaining to a core issue can be collected (without the influence of dominant personalities) and categorised into groups of ideas that are similar.

Why?

- To correctly identify the elements in a problematic situation.
- To reduce a complex situation into manageable parts.
- To create a foundation from which new ideas may be generated.

When?

- When a little right-brain input is needed to balance the left-brain input.
- At various stages of the process, but mostly for **A**lternatives in CIGARS.

Who?

- Affinity Diagrams is a team activity. Include people who have knowledge of the subject being considered (but preferably from many different disciplines).

How?

- Appoint a facilitator to manage proceedings and enforce the rules.
- State the critical issue or question that the team has to consider (don't be too specific).
- With the central question in mind, each person in the group writes any number of ideas, with each idea written on a separate sticky note (e.g. *Post It* ® notes).
- Ideas must be clearly written in no more than 6 words.
- All ideas are then stuck onto a large whiteboard.
- Each participant in turn is called up and asked to review the ideas on the board.
- He/she must then rearrange the individual ideas into groupings that he/she feels comfortable with.

- This has to be done in silence – no pressure or suggestions from the rest of the team should be tolerated when a person is rearranging the ideas.
- Once the first member is finished, a second member is called up to do likewise.
- This carries on until all members are satisfied with the groupings.
- Eventually consensus will be reached as to the number of logical groups of ideas and the individual ideas within them.
- Agree on suitable titles for the various groups.
- Use as a basis for further ideas and for focusing work on constituent parts of a complex problem.

Association Words

What?
- Examines the links between random words and the issue for which a new idea is being sought.

Why?
- Forces one out of the monotony of conventional thinking patterns.
- Stimulates a consideration of new associations leading to more original ideas.

When?
- When searching for a new idea.
- The stage of Alternatives in CIGARS.

Who?
- Either by oneself or working in a group.

How?
- Take the list of words over the next two pages and randomly pick out a word.
- Alternatively you could randomly open a dictionary (or encyclopaedia) and point at a word while blindfolded.
- Now list as many things as you can think of with regard to the selected word (e.g. uses, attributes, features, characteristics, etc.)
- If you struggle, do not choose another word. Persevere with your chosen word.
- Once this is done force yourself to think of possible connections between each item on your list and the issue around which new ideas are needed.
- Write down all the similarities, no matter how bizarre.
- Repeat the process with another random word the next day (or a few days later) if you feel you've exhausted all possibilities.

Apple; Submarine; Horse; Volcano; London; Helicopter; Blue whale; US President; Barbed wire; Shaving cream; Garage; Cell phone; Lunchbox; Pay phone; Harley Davidson bike; Tintin; Scissors; Calculator; South Pole; Eiffel Tower; Nile River; Bulldog clip; Stapler; Briefcase; Lamp; Searchlight; Torpedo; Necktie; Underwear; Roof tiles; Envelope; Dictionary; Eagle; Giraffe; Snake; Walrus; Kayak; Iceberg; Microprocessor; Kettle; Journalist; Paint stripper; Charcoal; Aluminium; Dishcloth; Tennis racquet; Key; Hedge; Carpet; Hairbrush; United Nations; Banquet hall; Ticket; Flamethrower; Piston; Headrest; Boulder; Grass; Picture frame; Photograph; Stamp album; Balloon; Harbour; Banana; Amazon; Road sign; Aeroplane; General; Snowmobile; Cough mixture; Straw; Varnish; Satellite; Jupiter; Saturn; Moon; Mole; Glass bottle; Dinner jacket; Diary; Fountain pen; Beret; Propeller; Videotape; Nail file; Hammer; Aborigine; Chisel; Shark; Piranha; Crocodile; Kangaroo; Landmine; Trapeze; Bowling ball; Soccer ball; Bookcase; Orange; Eraser; Pencil; Fax machine; Bookmark; Alarm clock; Ruler; Magnifying glass; Rice; Telescope; Bus; Napoleon; Socrates; Comet; Black hole; Hovercraft; Steam train; Desk; Handcuffs; Rope; Belt; Shoes; Ladder; Tape recorder; Log cabin; Deck chair; Sun cream; Bowler hat; Bible; Glue; Bicycle; Curry; Wine; Beer; Whisky; Vodka; Tuna; Perfume; Einstein; Michelangelo; Traffic light; Roulette wheel; Tank; Shoelace; Swiss Army knife; Moses; Father Christmas; Antarctica; Fashion; Hydroplane; Coffee; Tin can; Abominable snowman; Marmalade; Leaf; Tunnel; Plastic bottle; Abacus; Casserole; Underground train; Poker; Fighter jet; Tripwire; Potter's wheel; Nail clipper; Shampoo; Silkworms; Butterfly; Postage stamp; Boomerang; Axe; Frisbee; Glider; Skidpan; Cannibal; Butler; Limousine; Stained-glass window; Cathedral; Washing line; Running shoes; Hydrogen; Newspaper; Radio; Television; Tarzan; Corkscrew; Guillotine; Pole vault; Glass marble; Bread; Milk; Sun; Tortoise; Parrot; Cable car; Parking bay; Supermarket trolley; Elastic band; Mars; Sewer; Toothpick; Comb; Dentist; Roadmap; Contact lens; Catapult; Pistol; Soap; Nailbrush; Duvet; Sleeping bag; Teacup; Helmut; Poodle; Granadilla; Scooter; Mirror; Goldfish; Seaweed; Parachute; Paris; Casino; Skateboard; Pier; Lighthouse; Whistle; Scarf; Goggles; Aqualung; F1 car; Smoke; Arch; Pavement; Octopus; Windmill; Monument; Termite; Chilli; Braces; Bungee; Toll road; Platform; Harpoon; Painting; Stopwatch; Salt; Custard; Tongue; Seatbelt; Spare wheel; Storeroom; Tractor; Cork; Statue; Light bulb; Meat pie; Green beans; Library; Laundry; Cash register; Skirt; Cooking pot; Crossbow; Ring; Ear; Radar; Recipe; Soup; Yacht; Truck; Castle; Pyramid; Neanderthal; Ghost; China; Tornado; Tides; Diamond; Gold; Battery; Canal; Shotgun; Wallpaper; Loudspeaker; Microphone; Dinghy; Shadow; Marathon; Sword; Crown; Velcro; Dinosaur; Valve;

Steel band; Triangle; Angel; Skyscraper; Broadway; Sailor; Farmer; Nurse; Teacher; Collie; Spiral binding; Fridge; Dustbin; Container; Crane; Bridge; Island; Taxes; Ejector seat; Dodo; Petal; Ostrich; Wigwam; Orchestra; Spanner; Factory; Saw; Chimney; Ceiling; Ink; Bayonet; Strawberry; Fingerprint; Glacier; Lifeboat; Violin; Trumpet; Flag; Sheep; Maize; Sand; Owl; Viking; Chess; Pipeline; Cave; Oyster; Beach; Umbrella; Magic; Airport; Dragon; Scenery; Peter Pan; Pharaoh; Fly fishing; Mafia; Piano; Necklace; Haystack; Fishnet; Boxing; Skeleton; Eclipse; Golf; Olympic Games; Elephant; Sock; Lawnmower; Oscar award; Eskimo; Spider; Pudding; Salad; Headache; Snooker; Starfish; Ivy; Daisy; Water; Candle; Match; Puzzle; Dice; Computer; Shopping bag; Picnic; Baton; Wetsuit; String; Ribbon; Gravestone; Bouquet; Clothes brush; Sugarcane; Beaver; Cheetah; Gate; Ice-cream; Chewing gum; Sail; Snowboard; Electric razor; Knight; Mosquito; Morse code; Braille; Mountain; Waterfall; Champagne; Cheese; Guard; Car wash; Grandparent; Coat; Boots; Pin; Havana cigar; Pirate; Monsoon; Jet-ski.

Brainstorming

What?

- A process by which either an individual or (more commonly) a team seeks out creative solutions to problems. In a group situation, the driving dynamic is the suspension of judgement.

Why?

- Freewheeling spontaneous ideas can lead to effective practical solutions.
- Combining and augmenting the creativity of many to arrive at new ideas.
- A deliberate attempt at creative thinking (i.e. forcing out the ideas).

When?

- When unusual solutions or ideas are being sought.
- The Alternatives stage in CIGARS.

Who?

- Individuals working alone tend to generate more ideas than teams do.
- The ideas from a team brainstorm may be fewer, but they are likely to be better developed. Optimal group size for a brainstorm is 5–7 participants.

How?

- Nominate an effective facilitator who can:
  - prevent the usual people from dominating proceedings
  - effectively eliminate any criticism of ideas
  - encourage everyone to participate
  - keep the discussion focused on the subject/issue.
- Choose team members from a number of different disciplines. Ensure that each will have something constructive to contribute.
- Inform everyone of the fixed time period for the duration of the session.
- The issue that the team should address must be clear and well defined.

- Allow participants to spontaneously suggest ideas. This can be done either at random or in order around a table (members can opt to pass on their turn if they haven't a contribution at that particular moment).
- Make sure that each idea is properly recorded preferably on flipcharts so all can see the ideas. Don't give the recording task to the facilitator.
- All discussions should be conducted in a fun atmosphere. Abnormal and unusual ideas are to be welcomed just as much as sensible and conventional ones.
- Build on the ideas of others and try and generate as many ideas as possible.
- The facilitator should also keep an eye on the time and ultimately try and steer discussions towards the development of practical solutions.

Some find that the most effective method is individual first, followed by group. The members are first given the problem and asked to develop as many possible solutions on their own. These are all brought to the group brainstorm where they are made available to everyone (anonymity of ideas is observed). These are the raw materials for the group brainstorm where ideas are combined and further developed.

See also Nominal Group Technique (below).

Comic Relief

What?

- A team activity where participants think up humorous comments to situations depicted in pictures.

Why?

- To gauge the underlying and unspoken sentiments within a company.
- A fun team activity for problem-solving teams.

When?

- If staff members are reluctant to express their true opinions.
- Trying to identify the some of the problems within the company.
- The Circumstances and Impediment stages in CIGARS.

Who?

- Members of staff who may be reluctant to express their true thoughts.

How?

- More a humorous pastime than a problem-solving technique, Comic Relief can assist in identifying under-the-surface issues within a firm.
- As preparation you need to cut out numerous photos from newspapers or magazines. Try and select pictures that feature unusual facial expressions, action shots, conflicts, funny situations, etc. Photojournalists are good at catching such shots.
- Trim off any descriptors to the picture (i.e. only the picture itself should remain).
- For better handling it is good to glue the pictures to a piece of clean white board.
- On the day of the meeting break the team into sub-groups of 3 or 4 people.
- Give each small group a number of the pictures (pick a few at random) and ask each group to add humorous comments to their pictures. These can either be descriptors (at the bottom) or bubbles (speech or thought) for the characters.

- Each team should try and make the humour relevant to the company and/or its managers/employees.
- Participants should avoid scathing or harsh humour, but poking fun at some of the quirky habits of people or the management is within the spirit of the exercise.
- Teams can share their contributions with others to add to the fun of the occasion.
- Team members need to be assured of anonymity once the completed pictures are collected for review.

Decision Trees

What?

- A diagram that shows the choices and the outcomes that one faces under certain circumstances. The diagram also shows the chain of events likely to result from particular decisions.

Why?

- An effective analytical tool for evaluating different decisions and their implications.
- To reduce complex scenarios into a logical picture where all existing information can be used to arrive at the best decision.

When?

- When a lot of complex information needs to be taken into account.
- When seeking the optimal decision amongst different alternatives.
- The Select stage in CIGARS.

Who?

- Either individual or group. As this is very much a left-brain exercise, it probably best suits the individual.

How?

- State the problem or the major decision that needs to be made.
- Identify the major alternatives that are possible out of this decision or problem.
- Make sure that all of these alternatives are exhaustive (i.e. there aren't any you haven't considered).
- Represent the initial decision by means of a small square on the left hand side of a page or whiteboard (NB draw it half-way between the top and bottom).
- Now draw equidistant branches to the right representing every alternative or possible solution that had been considered.
- If these subsequent states are new decision points, represent each by means of a square. If they are uncertain or random states (i.e. outside of your control) represent each by means of a circle.

- Carry on constructing the tree showing all the important scenarios.
- Make sure that all decision events are mutually exclusive. In other words if you choose one branch, you can't choose another as well.
- If a decision is called for at one of the nodes, make sure that all possible outcomes are represented.
- Once all the possible scenarios have been drawn into the diagram, the next step is to assign probabilities to the various branches in the tree. Sometimes these values are a consensus view from participants familiar with the process.
- End values at the end of each branch may also be included. By combining the end values with the respective probabilities (i.e. multiplying them) one can work from the right of the diagram towards the left to determine which alternative is likely to be optimal (see the example on the next page).

Example of a Decision Tree

Company A has an agent to handle and represent all of its business in Finland. The agent accepts all costs incurred in marketing A's product in that country and in return is allowed to retain 75% of the gross revenue generated each year. Company A is considering terminating the agency agreement and assuming responsibility for its own business in Finland. For this, it will need to invest in its own subsidiary operation and here it has a choice of two alternatives. It can choose either a large operation (with an annual operating cost of $ 450k) or a medium operation (with an annual cost of $ 350k). The medium-sized operation is limited in that it can only handle up to a maximum of $ 750k p.a. in terms of revenue. Company A has also received three general forecasts for the economy over the next few years. A strong market is forecasted with a probability of 0.2, an average market with a probability of 0.5 and a weak market with a 0.3 probability, with revenue for Company A's product expected to be $ 1 500k, $ 500k and $ 300k respectively. These forecasts apply to every decision alternative. What should Company A do?

The problem can be represented and assessed in a decision tree:

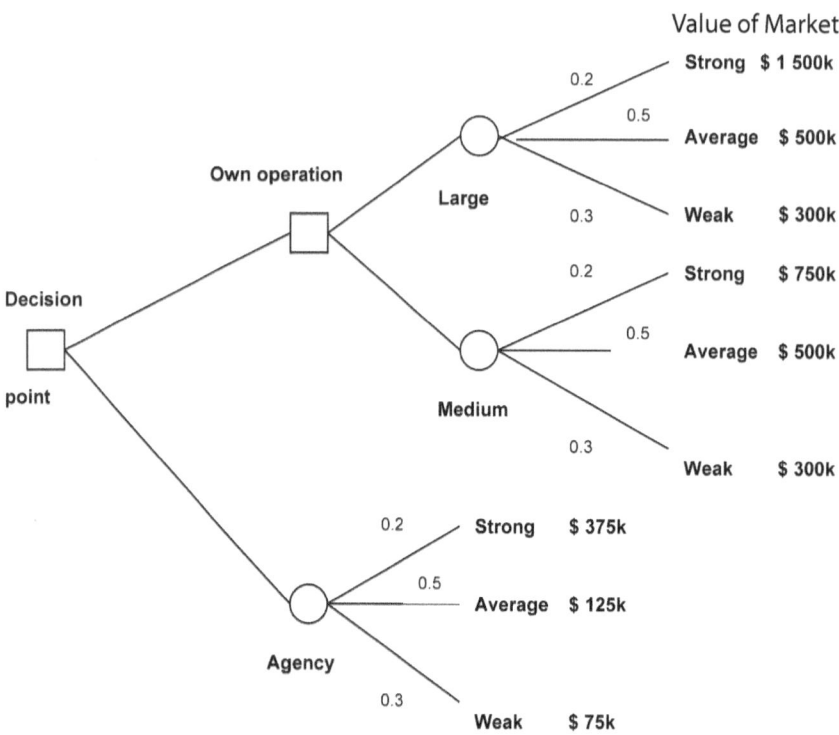

Can you see how the end values in each alternative were derived? The revenue from the medium operation is limited to a maximum of $ 750k p.a. and A only receives 25% of gross revenues in the agency alternative. In each branch of the tree the values are calculated from the right to the left. Each end value is multiplied with the relevant probability factor and the products are then summed for each discrete case. The net values of each alternative can be determined as, Large office $ 190k, Medium office $ 140k and Agency $ 160k. So the large office looks best. But the question that Company A needs to ask is whether the effort and risk in establishing this new office is worth the additional income of $ 30k p.a.?

Fishbone Diagram

What?

- A diagram that shows all the underlying causes of a problem. So named because it looks like the backbone of a fish. Also known as a cause and effect diagram.

Why?

- Useful method for representing/identifying the causes of a problem.
- Allows analysis of underlying causes and to see where the best potential for remedial action will give the highest return.

When?

- Where the possible underlying causes for a problem are suspected to be more than one.
- When diagnosing a problem.
- The **C**ircumstances and **I**mpediment stages in CIGARS.

Who?

- Individual or team. A team of people familiar with the problem is best.

How?

- Gather the relevant team of people into a meeting.
- State the basic problem in simple clear terms and ensure everyone agrees that this is the root problem.
- Write the problem down on the right-hand side (in the middle) of a large whiteboard.
- Draw a horizontal line across the board to the left of the stated problem. This is the spine of the fish. From the spine, draw off lines at 60° angles (see diagram on next page) to form the bones of the fish.
- At the end of each bone, write down a cause for the problem that you stated at the head. Get the team to contribute in identifying all the likely causes.
- It might be a good idea to initially write each cause on a *Post It* ® sticker. This allows you to rearrange the causes either in similar groups or in some other logical structure once they have all been recorded.

- Some people recommend that the more significant causes should be placed closer to the head of the fish with the lesser ones being located towards the tail.
- You may need to summarise some of the causes into one headline cause. For this purpose you can even decide to start separate secondary fishbone diagrams.
- One of the benefits of this method is that one avoids managers getting locked onto one particular cause. It is also useful in exposing causes that might otherwise have remained unspoken and it can aid in prioritising tasks.
- Probably the greatest value comes in the production of the diagram itself. In going through the process, the seeds of new ideas and insights are born. People also get a good appreciation of where the immediate actions need to be focused.

Example of a Fishbone Diagram

Let us assume that the management of an organisation has a problem with high staff absenteeism. In a meeting called to discuss the problem, the team soon realises that absenteeism is only a symptom. The core problem is low staff morale. This is then used as the root problem and the possible causes are listed in a fishbone diagram:

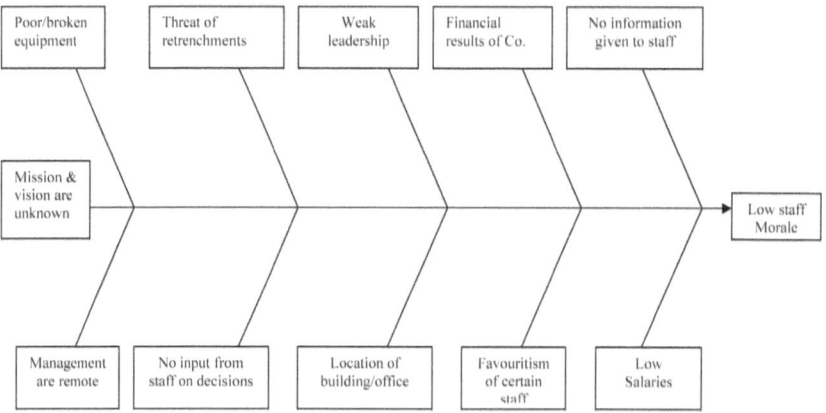

This diagram might then be modified into a more logical one like the one below:

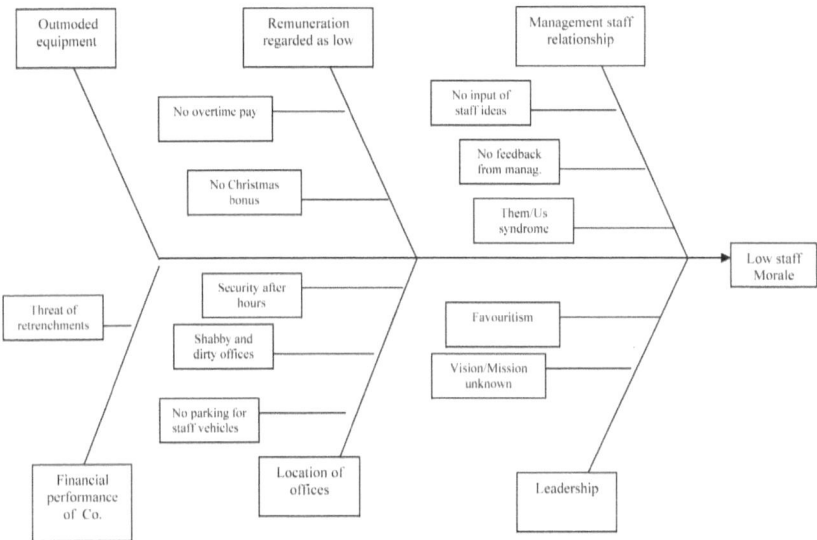

Five Whys

What?
- A method for probing a situation to identify the core problem.

Why?
- To ensure that the true problem is correctly identified.
- A safeguard against individuals or teams assuming things that don't exist.

When?
- When you suspect that symptoms are being misconstrued as problems.
- The **C**ircumstances and **I**mpediment stages in CIGARS.

Who?
- Either individually or within problem-solving teams. The latter will give a greater balance of views.

How?
- Begin by stating your problematic situation.
- Ask why this situation has occurred. You are looking for a single prime cause, not a number of influencing factors.
- Answer the initial question.
- Now ask why this underlying factor has occurred.
- Again answer the question in simple direct terms.
- Keep repeating the process until asking 'why' again seems fruitless. Some say this 'dead-end' will normally be reached after asking 'why' five times – hence the name.
- The last answer will be the root problem.

Many people regard the Five Whys technique as rudimentary. Perhaps its simplicity is its greatest strength (see Occam's Razor below). It is only really useful where there is a single contributing cause to the problem. But in many everyday business situations, too many things are assumed and too few things are questioned by the various participants. The Five Whys is an attempt to challenge that view. It may not resolve your situation, but it can help in identifying the real impediment. In terms of an application, rather than having one large group attempting the exercise, try breaking the group into a number of smaller independent groups. Each team could then be given the same initial question and told to apply the Five Whys technique. This tends to result in a number of interesting and divergent views which can then be collated and assimilated into one overall assessment.

Example of the Five Whys

A company wishes to understand why its sales were significantly below budget in the previous month. It begins by stating the problem:

Sales were 15% below target last month.

Why?
- The standing order to Argyle & Co. (major customer) was not processed.

Why?
- The order was shipped, but was returned to the factory.

Why?
- The dispatch department had not adhered to Argyle's new specifications for its shipment's packaging.

Why?
- The request had not been captured in the dispatching system.

Why?
- Client services (which deals directly with Argyle) does not have access to the computerised dispatching system. The requested changes had been relayed to the dispatch department through e-mail, but the instruction had been overlooked.

We could go on asking why, but it won't be that constructive. It now appears as if the problem was (and is) the dispatching system and its inability to interface with the systems managed by the client services department.

Flowcharts

What?
- A tool that breaks a process down into individual activities and then arranges them in a logical order so that one can understand the relationships between the various events.

Why?
- Gives a comprehensive understanding of a process very efficiently.
- Allows one to pinpoint potentially problematic steps or areas for improvement.

When?
- When an understanding of a complex process needs to be gained.
- When communicating a process to others in the organisation.
- The Circumstances and Impediment stages in CIGARS.

Who?
- Individual or team. A flowchart complied in a team setting can be very efficient if the members are appropriately chosen for their knowledge and experience.

How?
- Each flowchart is unique to its situation, but here are a few general guidelines:
- Begin by stating the title of the process that is being charted.
- Consider how the process begins – what triggers the events to take place? Make this the first box and describe the event (within the box) as briefly as possible without its meaning appearing unclear.
- Note each successive event and describe each in a similar manner. Connect each of the boxes in a sequential manner with an arrowed line.
- At times the flowchart may branch into a number of alternatives. Try and avoid complicating the chart with too much complexity. Decide which of the alternatives is the main flow of the process and retain that branch on the main diagram.

The secondary branches can refer to separate flowcharts that illustrate the various subroutines.

- Continue identifying and describing each sequential event until the process reaches a conclusion.
- Different symbols are usually used for different operations. These are:

  an event that is controlled within the process (the most common box)

  an event that occurs automatically

  a decision point in the process (e.g. a question with Yes/No branches)

  to mark the point where the flowchart connects with another process

- But concentrate rather on describing the process accurately. That's more important than using the symbols correctly!

Example of a Flowchart

I've purposely selected a simplistic example to illustrate how easy it is to break a process down into all the sequential events. A flowchart may be a fairly rudimentary tool, but it's useful in getting a common understanding as to the flow of activities.

Flowchart for taking the car out of the garage

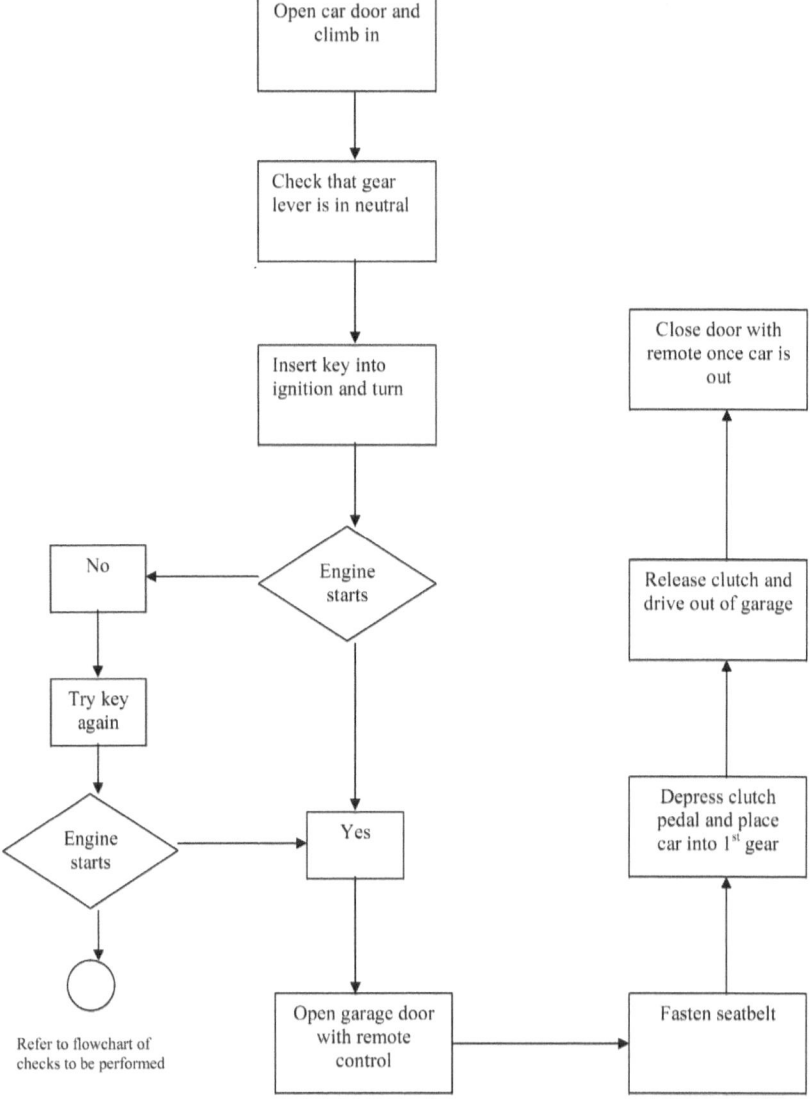

Force Field Analysis

What?
- Identifying the factors that are positive influences on a problem and those that are negative influences. Thereafter determining action plans that will increase the effects of the positive factors and reduce those of the negative ones.

Why?
- Recognises that a number of factors can be brought to bear on a complication.
- A multi-dimensional approach that increases the probability of success (i.e. not having to rely on a single solution).

When?
- At times when change is needed in an organisation.
- When there's a need to uncover all the relevant factors around an issue.
- To determine an appropriate action plan to resolve the complication.
- The Select and Implement stages in CIGARS

Who?
- Either an individual or a team. A team is more effective in identifying all the relevant factors as well as gaining ideas on how to improve the situation.

How?
- Write the problem or issue in a box in the middle of a whiteboard.
- On the left-hand side of the box list all the factors that will contribute positively to the issue under review.
- On the right-hand side of the box list all the factors that are negative influences on (or forces against) the issue.
- You may need to brainstorm these as some people may disagree as to what are positive and negative factors.
- Score each of the factors in terms of its strength from 1 (weak) to 5 (strong).
- Draw a force field diagram showing the forces and the size of each (see diagram on next page).

- The total scores for the positive and negative influences will give an indication of the viability of the project or the issue needing to be changed.
- In order to move forward one should either reduce the strength of the opposing forces, increase the strength of the positive forces or, best of all, implement a combination of both.
- Concentrate first on those forces that are perceived to be the strongest.
- Bear in mind that it is sometimes easier to reduce the effects of negative forces than it is to increase the effect of positive ones.
- Determine specific action plans for each force identified for change (i.e. measurable objectives, deadlines, responsibilities, etc.).

Example of a Force Field Analysis

A business is considering changing from its current situation where it makes all deliveries to customers to one where it would outsource this function to an outside delivery company. The forces for and against this change are shown in the Force Field diagram below:

In our example, because the negative forces outweigh the positive ones, one might assume that the idea or project is not viable. This would be incorrect. Further work needs to done. For instance, the company tendering for the business may be prepared to brand its delivery vans with the company's brands and logos. It may be possible for the company's drivers and maintenance staff to be transferred to the contracting company on the same benefits that they enjoy today. Service level agreements can provide comfort in terms of maintaining customer service levels. All of these would reduce the negative forces and make the change easier.

But force field analysis is not limited to cases where changes are being considered. It can be used in a number of different situations. Very often a problem or impediment can be countered on a number of fronts. Some of these involve reducing the negative effects of some factors while others call for greater impetus on forces that contribute positively to the problem. In these applications, force field analysis is a useful tool.

Lateral Thinking

What?

- Much cited (but less explained) method of considering a problem from a novel angle. Very basically, a way of generating new ideas that is outside the bounds of conventional logic.

Why?

- New ideas often come from unusual perception points.
- To break away from the rigidity of traditional reasoning (vertical thinking).
- To explore multiple possibilities rather than relying on a single approach.

When?

- When generative rather than selective thinking is needed.
- The **A**lternatives stage in CIGARS.

Who?

- Either individuals or groups. But in many cases group pressure can restrict the lateral thinking potential.

How?

- The first step in lateral thinking is to recognise that you need to escape from the jail that imprisons your mind. You need to move across (laterally) to a new vantage point where the governing rule is perception, not logic.
- Ask open-ended questions like 'How?' and 'Why?' instead of specific questions that are likely to lead to certain conclusions based on traditional logic.
- Be aware of your current thinking around the problem. In most cases where a problem is being analysed, greater activity results in your getting deeper and deeper in a particular direction (like digging a deeper hole when what you really seek is a new one in a different location).
- Drilling is a good metaphor for vertical thinking. For lateral thinking, the metaphor would be skating or skimming. Let's illustrate this with a story: Imagine yourself on a frozen lake. Somewhere beneath the ice is a massive shoal of fish. You have already drilled one hole through the ice to catch these fish, but with limited success. Some are suggesting that we make

the present hole bigger in order to introduce more lures and lines. A lateral thinker decides to disregard the current hole, put her skates on, and skate around the surface of the lake. While enjoying this exercise, she 'comes across' something that leads to the location of the fish. Once the new successful fishing site has been established, the vertical thinkers will all be able to show you how it was just a matter of time before they too would have discovered it. Logic can always find the rationale for a solution, but sometimes it takes lateral thought to discover it. The keys to lateral thought are inquisitiveness and an open mind, not logic and analysis.

Lateral thinking is essentially a synonym for creative thought. Many workshops where people are supposed to be thinking 'laterally' quickly degenerate into exercises in vertical thinking. Be aware of these differences.

Lotus Blossom Technique

What?
- A novel method of generating new ideas around a central theme or problem.

Why?
- Recognises that ideas tend to build upon each other.
- A practical mechanism for recording the free-flowing mind.

When?
- When further new ideas regarding a problem or issue are needed.
- The Alternative stage in CIGARS.

Who?
- Like many techniques it can be used individually, but a group is likely to generate more ideas.

How?
- Using the diagram on the next page as a template, draw the schematic onto a whiteboard in the meeting room.
- Write the central theme, idea or issue in the small box at the very centre of the diagram.
- Ask the group to think of eight ideas, solutions or applications that are related to the issue written at the centre.
- These are then written in the boxes surrounding the central box (see the diagram).
- These eight themes are then copied into the centres of the boxes surrounding the box in the middle.
- Now, taking each periphery box in turn, generate a further eight ideas around each central issue.
- The group may struggle to fill every available box. If so, move on to the next issue. Try and fill as many of the boxes as possible.
- Evaluate and discuss the resulting ideas.

Example of a Lotus Blossom Technique
Let us assume the same issue that confronted us in the Fishbone diagram case, low staff morale. This is written in the very centre box and the group brainstorms related issues. These related items or causes are written around

the core problem before being transferred to the middle of the 'outer petals' of the lotus blossom. The exercise would look something like this:

	Manag.			Salaries			Poor equip.	
			Manag.	Salaries	Poor equip.			
Staff benefits			Staff benefits	**Low staff morale**	Building		Building	
			Staff function	Threat of job loss	Staff share scheme			
	Staff function			Threat of job loss			Staff share scheme	

In the exercise above, the group identified management, low salaries, poor equipment, office building, a staff share scheme, the threat of job loss, staff functions and other staff benefits as being eight issues related to the core problem of low morale. Each one of the eight then becomes a core seed for a further eight ideas in an outer box. When the exercise is complete, all the ideas are discussed and considered for possible implementation.

Matrix

What?

- Simplifying a problem by representing it in a grid of cells (the number depends upon the problem itself). Basically, a structuring tool that sorts information into a format that makes it easy to analyse.

Why?

- Simplifies a problem into its core elements.
- Allows one to identify connections or correlations between factors.
- Reduces the complexity of language.

When?

- When the relationship between factors needs to be considered and assessed.
- When the information being analysed lends itself to categorisation.
- The Circumstances stage of CIGARS.

Who?

- Either an individual or a group.

How?

- Every matrix is different since it is determined by the problem in question.
- Identify the factors or elements of the problem.
- Identify the possible outcomes for each element.
- Construct a matrix where all the elements are listed down the first column and the outcomes are listed along the top row (see the example on the next page)
- Analyse each situation separately (i.e. the intersection of each row and column)

The matrix is one of the simplest problem-solving techniques, but it is also one of the most effective. The human mind often battles with a problem when it is presented in words and sentences. Once the essential information is summarised into a matrix the solution often becomes obvious. It is one of those techniques where practice makes perfect and the more you apply it the more you will come to rely upon it. It can be used effectively in many problem situations. For instance, the example illustrating Decision Trees (the business in Finland) could also have been analysed by means of a matrix.

But look at the example on this page and start trying to structure your everyday work problems into a matrix format. There really is no special trick to it – it is simply an effective way of setting out a problem so that it can be considered objectively.

Example of a Matrix
Magic Metals (Pty) Ltd manufacture screws and bolts for industrial applications. The quality control (QC) department tests each batch for defects. These fall into three categories: flaking, discolouration and cracking. The number of customer complaints has been increasing over the last few months and the company wishes to identify the cause and fix it. Records from the QC office over the last six months seem to indicate that the most common fault detected is discolouration (245 cases). Next come flaking (66 cases) and cracking (29 cases). The company relies on three different suppliers (A, B & C) for its raw materials. Of the metal supplied by Company A, there were 19 flaking, 75 discolouration and 5 cracking defects. Metal from supplier B showed 35 flaking, 140 discolouration and 9 cracking defects. In the case of supplier C, the flaking defects totalled 12, the discolouration 30 and the cracking 16. The QC office have also informed us that over the same period the number of batches that were purchased from A, B and C were 2 000, 5 000 and 1 000 respectively.

Matrix No. 1: Number of defects per supplier

	No. of flaking defects	No. of discolouration defects	No. of cracking defects
Supplier A	19	75	5
Supplier B	35	140	9
Supplier C	12	30	16
Total defects	66	245	30

The matrix certainly sets out the information in a more lucid manner, but it still doesn't tell us much. We might even infer that discolouration is the number one problem and that supplier B seems to be source for most of the defects. But a more accurate picture will emerge if we take into account the relative quantities purchased from each supplier. We know that 2 000 batches were from supplier A, 5 000 from B and 1 000 from C.

Calculating the defects as percentages of the original batches and placing these in a matrix is much more revealing:

Matrix No. 2: Percentage defects per supplier

	% of flaking defects	% of discolouration defects	% of cracking defects
Supplier A	1.0%	3.8%	0.3%
Supplier B	0.7%	2.8%	0.2%
Supplier C	1.2%	3.0%	1.6%

Immediately one can see that the percentage of cracking defects with regard to supplier C is substantially higher than it is for the other two suppliers – in fact it is more than five times higher. All the other percentages are fairly constant. You subsequently learn that cracking defects are by far the most serious since screws and bolts suffering these defects are totally unusable. In other words, these defects are much more likely to lead to customer complaints than either flaking or discolouration. From this matrix it looks likely (but not certain) that the cause of complaints may have something to do with the raw materials that are being sourced from supplier C. In this case the matrix has helped establish your first area of investigation.

Mind Maps®

What?

- A method of depicting a problem (or issue) that links it to numerous related ideas and concepts through the use of symbols, diagrams, images, colours and words. Mind Maps® was created by acclaimed author and creativity expert Tony Buzan.

Why?

- A schematic that is closer in structure to the thought patterns of your mind (i.e. not bound by a strict logical order).
- Uses drawings, images and colours as well as words (a conduit for right-brain thinking).

When?

- When creative right-brain thinking is required.
- When connections between pieces of information are being sought.
- To identify all the issues and sub-issues around a problem as well as solutions.
- In the **C**ircumstances and **A**lternatives stages of CIGARS.

Who?

- A Mind Map® is like trying to sketch one's thought processes while thinking around a problem; it is therefore an exercise that better suits the individual. In a meeting it can be effective in recording the group's discussions and findings.

How?

- Use a large piece of blank white paper – turn it sideways (landscape format)
- State the problem or issue in a bubble in the centre of the page (if you can illustrate the problem with a drawing instead of a bubble, so much the better)
- Beginning with this central issue, think of as many related concepts and ideas as you can. See every new idea as separate train of thought and represent each by means of a branch radiating from the centre core.
- You don't have to work in any order – allow the map to record your brain's thinking patterns. You may want to think firstly

about all the concepts and ideas related to the core issue (i.e. the main branches), with the development of each idea into sub-branches being left as a secondary exercise. Or you may wish to develop each individual branch into numerous sub-branches before you consider another idea that stems directly from the centre point. Whatever suits you is fine.

- Use different colours for different branches. It helps to stimulate creative thought.
- Avoid the use of sentences. Use key words only and print these neatly along the branches of the map (or in bubbles at the end of each branch). Where possible, try and use images, sketches and symbols to illustrate the concepts.
- Now look at the map as a whole. Draw in all necessary connections between the various ideas and elements.
- Study the map to explore new interrelationships and identify new solutions.

Example of a Mind Map®

I have used the main issues covered in the section entitled *Rediscovering Your Creative Ability* to illustrate the use of this tool on the next page.

Mind Map for Creativity

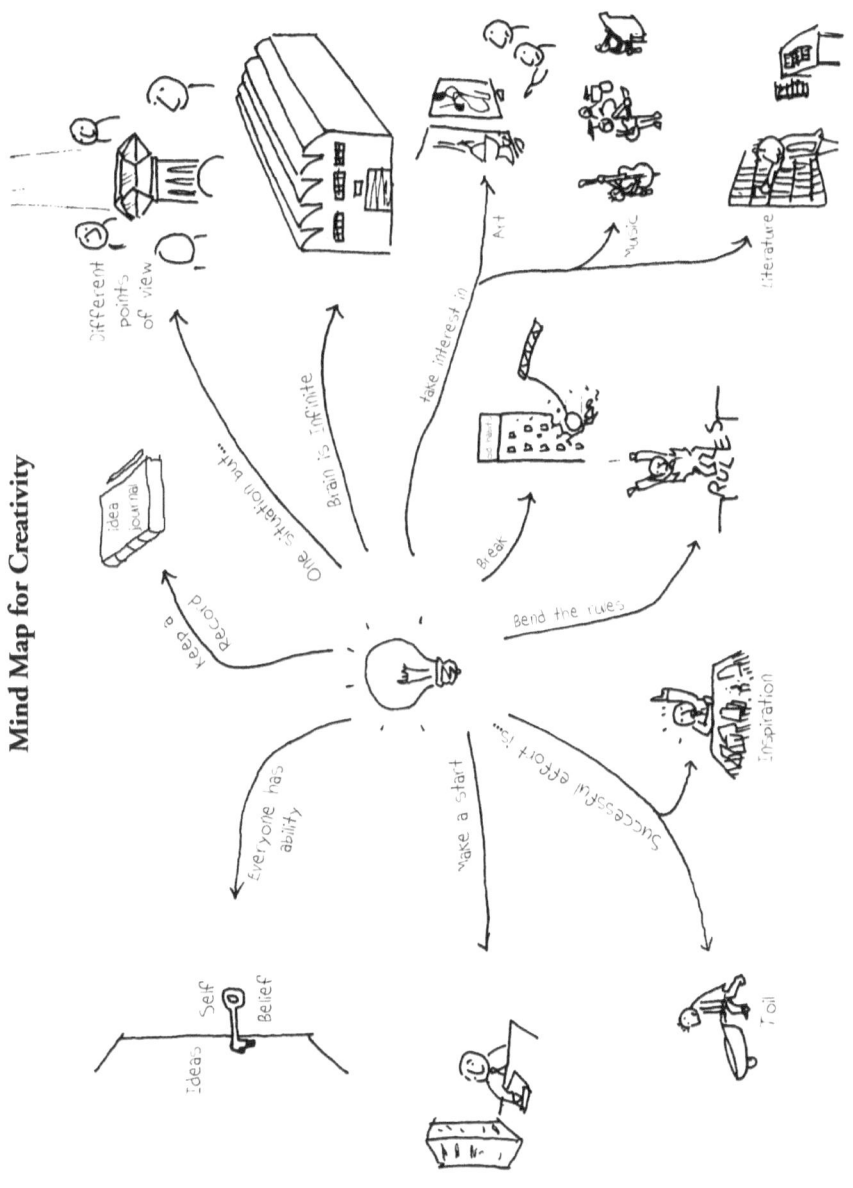

Nominal Group Technique

What?

- A method used within brainstorming to ensure that dominant or assertive personalities do not unduly influence the work of the group.

Why?

- Leaders or others in authority tend to have an inordinate say in brainstorming outcomes. This technique ensures that all participants have equal influence.
- Sometimes the quieter, less effusive, people in a business have good ideas. It is important that these ideas or solutions are given a platform for consideration.

When?

- When a group needs to make a decision.
- To establish the priorities in a problem situation.
- The **A**lternatives and **S**elect stages in CIGARS.

Who?

- As with brainstorming, a team of 6–12 people.

How?

- Many of the procedures for conducting a brainstorm apply here with the following adaptations:
- After writing the problem on a whiteboard (or similar), the leader asks the members to write down their suggestions in terms of solutions or ideas. This is done in silence over a period of 5–10 minutes. No comments between members should be tolerated.
- After this the leader goes around the table and asks each member for his or her first idea. These are then recorded. This procedure is repeated for every member's second idea and so on. Once a member has no more ideas he/she simply passes when asked for input. This continues until all the ideas from the group have been recorded on the whiteboard (i.e. everyone passes on the round robin).
- The leader then reviews each idea in turn so that everyone in the group understands what is meant by the stated solution/ idea. If any item needs further clarification, the person who

proposed it can explain the point, but not promote it. One way of achieving this is to limit each person's explanation of his or her idea to 20 seconds.

- Thereafter the leader asks each member to vote for the best solutions. This is done anonymously on white cards that are collected by the leader once each member has voted.
- There may be a need for two or three rounds of voting, depending on the number of issues or ideas generated. For example, if 50 issues are initially listed, the leader could ask everyone to first pick their top ten. Thereafter the top five could be voted from a reduced list of around 20. Finally, with the voting list being reduced to ten, members could vote on their top three.

Problem Definition

What?
- A group technique used to ensure that the key problem or impediment is correctly identified.

Why?
- In practice the solutions to business problems often fail because the problem was not clear or the solution was focused in the wrong area. Problem definition can avoid these pitfalls.
- Different people have different views on problems. Tapping into these divergent views can lead to a better understanding especially of a complex situation.

When?
- When the underlying problem is not apparent.
- When many different viewpoints on a situation are needed.
- The **C**ircumstances and **I**mpediment stages in CIGARS.

Who?
- Ideally participants who have either a direct or an indirect link to the circumstances.

How?
- Discuss the overall situation within the group.
- Make bullet points of the key characteristics, features and issues.
- List all the critical players in the scenario (i.e. everyone with an interest – direct or indirect – in seeing a satisfactory outcome).
- What would the main players like to avoid or reduce?
- What would the main players like to increase or receive in abundance?
- What are the other critical factors in the environment?
- Write down a first draft of the problem statement.
- Critically discuss this within the group. Ask for alternative definitions. Discuss these.
- Establish the points of agreement and the various differences. Resolve the latter.
- Agree on a final definition of the problem.

- Ensure that the definition is SIMPLE, BALANCES the interests of the various stakeholders and is SPECIFIC enough to ensure appropriate focus.

Pros, Cons & Fixes

What?

- Analysing a situation into its positives and negatives with scrutiny of the latter to see which can be reduced or disregarded.

Why?

- To counter the tendency that people have for negative thinking.
- To increase the probability of a finding a positive solution.

When?

- When considering a choice between alternatives.
- When a decision or way forward is required.
- The **C**ircumstances and **R**eview stages in CIGARS.

Who?

- A team of people familiar with the problem is best.

How?

- List all the positive characteristics (the pros) of each alternative.
- Now list all the negative aspects (the cons). This list tends to be longer than the first.
- Working with the list of cons, combine those that are essentially the same (people have a tendency to see the same negatives in different ways). Also consider which of the cons could be eliminated on the grounds of being subjective or irrelevant to the problem under consideration.
- Taking each of the cons on the reduced list in turn, think of ways in which each can be rectified or fixed. Ask how you can convert the con into a pro. Even a partial transformation or reduction is good. This is similar to a brainstorm exercise – first seek out as many fixes for each con as possible. When you've exhausted all ideas, only then consider which are practical in each case.
- Now rewrite the lists of pros as well as those cons that can't be eliminated.
- Compare pros and unavoidable cons of each alternative and make a decision.

Example of Pros, Cons & Fixes

A manufacturing business is considering investing in a new machine that will increase productivity and ultimately lower the unit cost of production.

Step 1: List the Pros

Pros
- Reduced costs of production
- Staff headcount reduced
- Less pressure from unions
- Less disruptions and stoppages
- Easier to meet high season demand

Step 2: List the Cons

Cons
- Greater capital investment
- Servicing and maintenance will increase
- Need to secure new supplier for raw material
- Current production levels do not justify cost reduction
- Staff unfamiliar with new machine
- Limits flexibility
- Reputation of machine is untested (not many other users in market)
- High production output will lead to bottlenecks in plant
- Viability is totally dependent upon demand for one product
- Fixed costs will increase
- Risks are increased
- Power consumed will increase
- Machine will replace staff who have long service with the company

Step 3: Reduce/convert the cons

Review Cons
- Greater capital investment (fact – can't neutralise this)
- Servicing and maintenance will increase (but production costs will be reduced – drop)
- Need to secure new supplier for raw material (are there no suitable suppliers? – drop)
- Current production levels do not justify cost reduction (true, but in the future they will be)
- Staff unfamiliar with new machine (true – but training will eliminate this)
- Limits flexibility (fact – can't neutralise this)
- Reputation of machine is untested (if our engineers approve, it must be OK –drop)
- High production output will lead to bottlenecks in plant (production planning -drop)
- Viability is totally dependent upon demand for one product (combine with risks)
- Fixed costs will increase (but overall production costs will be reduced. Keep because it may have implications on break-even point)
- Risks are increased (Combined with dependency)
- Power consumed will increase (irrelevant – production costs will decrease – drop)
- Machine will replace staff who have long service with the company (sentimental – drop)

The company can reduce the list of cons to five, and two of these (current production not justifying cost reduction and fixed costs increasing) could really only be counted as half issues. Now the cons do not outweigh the pros and a positive decision looks more likely. When comparing different alternative solutions, the exercise above should be performed for each alternative. Once each of the lists of pros and cons has been reduced or consolidated, it is easier to identify the best alternative.

Reversing the Problem

What?
- Deliberately focusing on the opposite of an issue or problem to identify a solution or idea that would normally not have been considered.

Why?
- To counter against the 'silo' effects of left-brain thinking.
- To challenge the logic and conclusions of a particular solution.
- The belief that everything in the world has an opposite. By focusing on this, one gains a better understanding of the primary issue or concept.

When?
- When a fresh approach or new ideas are needed.
- To ensure that nothing has been overlooked in a proposed solution.
- The **A**lternatives and **R**eview stages in CIGARS.

Who?
- A team of people is most effective here, but an individual will also find the technique to be useful.

How?
- State the problem or issue as simply as possible.
- Now reword your statement into its complete opposite. For example if the problem is: How can we increase the visibility of our service in the market?, its opposite might be: What can we do to prevent people from hearing/learning about our service?
- List all the activities that could possible help in achieving the opposite statement.
- Consider the consequences of these actions. What could be the benefits of these results?
- Mind map the results or brainstorm any interesting ideas that can be further developed.
- Reversing a problem can also be applied to proposed solutions. Take the proposal, reverse it and subject it to the rigours of its converse. It can help to refine the end product.

Rival Hypotheses

What?
- Objectively considering a number of explanations (or hypotheses) as being possible causes of a particular set of circumstances.

Why?
- A number of hypotheses can explain a set of circumstances. To limit one's focus to one hypothesis can be risky.
- Reduces the risk of being emotionally attached to one hypothesis.

When?
- When an objective assessment of the situation is needed.
- The Circumstances stage in CIGARS.

Who?
- Either an individual or a problem-solving team.

How?
- The set of circumstances may suggest a particular explanation (hypothesis). However, there are many other hypotheses that could exist and still fit within the observed facts or evidence.
- Note your first or preferred hypothesis. Now consider any other possible causes for the current situation. Ask yourself what else could possibly account for the circumstances that you face.
- Don't dismiss a suggested hypothesis simply because you don't initially believe it. You will get a chance to test it along with the others.
- Draw up a matrix with all the individual facts or pieces of evidence from the circumstances listed separately in rows down the first column.
- Assign each of the rival hypotheses to the other columns of the matrix.
- Now consider each piece of evidence for every hypothesis in turn. Is this fact consistent or inconsistent with the hypothesis in question? Work through the matrix indicating an 'A' (for agrees) or a 'D' (for disagrees) for each hypothesis.
- The most likely hypothesis is **not** the one with the most A symbols, *but the one with the fewest D symbols*.

- Where the situation is inconclusive (very common in practice) remember that simpler explanations are preferred to more complex ones (see Occam's Razor below). Also more probable explanations are preferred to less probable ones.

Example of Rival Hypotheses

Tim Jones, MD of fast-food chain Cluckers Crispy Chicken (CCC) is concerned about the financial performance of his group. Last year's turnover was $ 66m (up 35% from $ 49m the previous year), but net profit has only increased by 9% from $ 4.5m to $ 4.9m. The company's product is proving to be very popular and the number of franchised stores grew from 62 at the beginning of the year to 95 by the close. Tim suspects that the relatively weak performance was the result of ineffective marketing. Almost 18 months ago the new marketing director switched to a new advertising agency. Since that date Tim has never really felt confident about the concepts and ideas that this new firm has introduced. And these radical ideas have come at a cost. Tim notices that marketing expenditure has increased by 56% from the previous year.

Tim's hypothesis: The marketing department is taking up an increasingly larger slice of the CCC cake. It has failed to translate its increased costs into a corresponding increase in turnover.

But Tim is cautious about possibly jumping to this conclusion and wishes to get a second opinion. He feels that the members in his management team may be slightly biased one way or the other and thus he seeks the advice of an outside consultant. The management consultant points out that there could be a number of reasons for the company's changed financial performance. Focusing on a single hypothesis can have the effect of shifting one's attention from other problematic areas whose symptoms may go unnoticed. The advisor proposes a number of rival hypotheses that, like the first, can be held up against certain key facts and observations to see whether the evidence refutes or supports the individual hypotheses.

They agree on the first hypothesis being:
- The marketing department has been inefficient in its use of resources over the last year

And devise the following rival hypotheses:
- The recent product changes (flavours and packaging) have not proved as popular as the features of the original product.

- Six months ago the economy started to cool down. Since then, discretionary incomes have been shrinking.
- The process of identifying and selecting sites for new franchisees over the last year was not as thorough as it has been in the past.
- The fast-food sector (particularly chicken) is one of the most competitive in the economy and the number of new entrants is amongst the highest of any industry.
- With the rapid growth in stores, training of new franchisees has been curtailed, resulting in a number of poorly managed businesses.

They would then work through all these alternatives seeing how well each fact in the company's circumstances agrees or disagrees with each hypothesis.

Useful Theories and Principles

These theories can be good guides when dealing with problems:

Occam's Razor

William of Ockham (Occam is the Latin spelling), an English philosopher in medieval times, is best remembered for the maxim known as Occam's razor. The statement that gave rise to his concept was, 'Plurality is not to be assumed without necessity'. In layperson's language what he meant was that, in any situation, the simplest explanation that fits the facts of the problem is the one that should be preferred. Don't complicate matters beyond what is necessary. Think how much time and effort would be saved in meetings if the chair applied Occam's razor to cut out all the absurdities, complexities and discussion of hypothetical concepts?

Of course, like everything else, the principle can be abused. There are circumstances where a simple explanation may not suffice and Occam did not suggest that complexity could always be reduced to simplicity. He believed that explanations should be based on the observable facts with logic being used to reach the conclusions. But if a number of models can equally explain the facts of a situation, Occam's razor will tell you that the simplest one is best. Don't multiply entities beyond what is necessary. And try not to forget it.

Pareto Analysis

Last century, an Italian economist, Vilfredo Pareto, developed laws on income distribution and in other socio-economic fields. His best-known law is more commonly known as *the 80-20 rule*. Basically the principle states that, in most activities, 80% of output is produced by 20% of the input. To illustrate the concept in business, one could translate it to: 80% of our company's turnover is generated by 20% of its products, or is dependent upon 20% of its clients. In most cases this general ratio is fairly accurate and it can be applied to numerous situations.

However, Pareto analysis can't be applied to all activities. Some are 'mission critical' and need to be performed 100% of the time. For example a surgeon has to ensure that all her operations are perfect. If she reserved her full attention for the 20% of her cases that provided 80% of her income, one or two failures due to negligence or a lapse in concentration would be disastrous. But the application of the theory is very useful when it comes to prioritising work. It's often not possible for a manager to spread his time evenly over all his required tasks. Sacrifice is sometimes the order of the day, and as things become more critical, so the focus needs to be intensified on the few things that are going to produce the biggest results.

Similarly, in problem solving you can use Pareto analysis to identify and prioritise your next steps. In many instances a number of issues will be contributing to a problematic situation. Not all of them can be addressed at the same time. But you can begin with the 20% that are probably making up 80% of the problem.

Parkinson's Law

Work expands to fill the time allocated for its completion. Devised by Professor Cyril Northcote Parkinson (1909–1993) as an observation (which some may describe as flippant and sarcastic) of the way people conduct their work. Unfortunately it appears to be quite an apt reflection, especially in bureaucratic organisations. As I mentioned earlier in the book, the reverse of Parkinson's Law is a good thing to consider when deciding upon a course of action. If work can expand to fill time available, it can equally be contracted if the amount of time is shrunk. So if your team estimates that a particular task will take four days to complete, set two days as their challenge.

Parkinson also came up with a number of other maxims (although none as celebrated as his first law), of which some are:
- Expenditure rises to meet income.
- Delay is the deadliest form of denial.
- Expansion means complexity, and complexity decay.
- Deliberative bodies become decreasingly effective after they pass five to eight members.

Crunchiness

The title of an article published in *The Economist* in August 1988 by Nico Colchester, the late deputy editor of that publication. Colchester felt that human prosperity followed a recurring cycle from crunchiness and wealth to sogginess and poverty. As he put it, 'Crunchiness brings wealth. Wealth leads to sogginess. Sogginess brings poverty. Poverty creates crunchiness.'

Crunchy systems are those where small changes have big results. There's an element of certainty with regard to crunchy systems – people are left in no doubt as to where they stand in the order of things or what the next steps are going to be. Crunchy things are on or off, 1 or 0, black or white, true or false, this or that, etc. Sogginess is the other extreme. Sogginess is described as comfortable uncertainty – it is similar to the grey zone of fuzzy logic. Colchester used fixed interest rates to illustrate a crunchy situation – both borrower and lender knew where they stood if the rates subsequently moved up or down. Floating interest rates on the other hand are soggy. He also used popular politicians from the eighties to illustrate the concepts. As I write, George W Bush is in his second term in office as the US President. He was re-elected ahead of his Democrat rival, John Kerry. Did the electorate perceive Bush as the crunchier candidate? I think they probably did.

Crunchy and soggy are more than just colourful adjectives. You can apply these universally self-intuitive descriptors to most arguments or proposals as a litmus test – 'is this a crunchy plan; if not, how do we remove the sogginess?' Most people have positive inclinations towards crunchy things and negative feelings towards soggy ones. Crunchy plans are almost always harder to achieve, but the results are more rewarding in terms of the goals and perhaps, a more galvanised team. Sogginess is the path of least resistance – avoid it if you want to make a real contribution. You'll find that not everything can be instantly transformed from soggy to crunchy, but adding these two words to your everyday vocabulary will help you see things for what they are.

Sunk-Cost Effect

I'm frequently amused at the number of times poker players will remain in the betting round even though they consider their hand to be a losing one. It's not the prospect of bluffing that's keeping them in the game – it's the amount of money that they've bet in that round ('I've put this much in the pot, I might as well see you'). They don't seem to understand that what they have laid out on the table, from the time they picked up their cards until the point when reality sinks in, is a sunk cost. This effect is also very common in business where people are loath to give up projects or ventures because of the time and effort that has been invested in them. When considering alternative solutions to a particular problem, people are often influenced by the sunk-cost effect. This can be countered by stressing the need to focus on and maximise future benefits rather than allowing past investments to dictate the destiny of the organisation.

Law of Contrasts

Our judgement is significantly influenced by what we have recently experienced. A person cooped up for hours in a stinking factory will be able to appreciate the sweet fragrance of a perfume more than someone who was previously subjected to neutral odours. If your previous boss was arrogant and demanding, you are likely to have an inflated opinion regarding your new boss with her placid manner. A sales forecast or budget may be well below the real potential because the team that prepared it based it on the below-par performances of previous years.

In problem solving, especially when working with others, consider what people might be using as their comparators. If your organisation has suffered a setback as a result of an abortive scheme, ask whether you are not overrating the new solution as a result of the previous fiasco. It sometimes needs the influence of an outsider before teams are able to appreciate issues in a more universal sense instead of one heavily influenced by recent experiences.

Chaos Theory

Over the years scientists have searched for the simplest views of the world in which we live (William of Ockham's influence?). Despite these efforts to predict and explain things, nature doesn't always behave in a deterministic way. Most of the world around us is actually chaotic. Weather forecasts, stock markets, populations, fluids in pipes, traffic flow, in fact almost anything that is subject to two or more forces, will tend to behave in a chaotic manner. And this chaos develops with time – at the outset the system often appears to be quite predictable. Scientists tend to define chaotic systems as those where a minute change in the initial variables will have a dramatic effect further down the line. The meteorologist Edward Lorenz likened it to a tornado in Texas resulting from the mere flap of butterfly's wings in Brazil.

Chaos theory is a fascinating subject, but it's beyond the scope of this book. From a problem-solving perspective, the main lesson is that most systems do not display a direct relationship between cause and effect. Business is a complex web of non-linear systems. You will not be able to control and predict all outcomes. Don't place too much reliance upon mathematical models or other analytical methods for solutions. At best you can identify and isolate the key variables and you can better understand how these interact, but you can't avoid risk and complexity. On the other hand, it would be foolish to disregard all analysis simply because predictability is uncertain. The person who seeks to understand the elements of a system will always be in a better position than the other who decries such efforts on the ground that things are better left to chance.

The Peter Principle

Perhaps even more tongue-in-cheek than Parkinson's Law, this principle states that, in every hierarchy, people will rise to their level of incompetence and will generally remain there. For example, the brightest and most talented mechanic will be earmarked as a team supervisor. If he is competent in this function, he will get prompted to workshop supervisor. Again if competent, he will become the garage manager. This will continue until he reaches a level where he's out of his depth – his level of incompetence. He will then have reached his ceiling for advancement. The corollary to this rule is that only those who have yet to reach their level of incompetence are capable of work. I suppose if you are considering the selection of effective members on your problem-solving team, favour those who have still to reach their level of incompetence!

The Turnpike Effect

Once something is put in place, or made available, its actual usage is far greater than was originally predicted. For instance the availability of a new photocopier in the accounts department is likely to increase its usage beyond the level currently estimated for that section. A rule of thumb for the turnpike effect is 15%. This is useful to bear in mind when considering new proposals.

Weighted Ranking

What?
- A technique for determining the preferences amongst a list of items according to objective criteria.

Why?
- Reduces the risk of emotion clouding a selection or choice.
- Ensures that the important criteria for a selection are taken into account and given the appropriate weighting.

When?
- When selecting a solution or alternative.
- To determine the ranking of a number of items or ideas.
- The **R**eview and **S**elect stages in CIGARS.

Who?
- A group or an individual. Greater buy-in will be achieved in a group application.

How?
- List the items that you need to rank.
- Determine the various criteria that may be taken into account when deciding on these items (e.g. cost, availability, warranty, flexibility, maintenance, etc).
- Create a matrix with the items listed down all the rows and across the columns. Blank out the redundant half of the matrix.
- Take the first criterion for selection – say for example it is cost. Label your matrix as Cost. Now work through this matrix pair-ranking each item against every other one according to cost. (See the example described in detail on page 45).
- Determine the ranking for all the items in terms of cost – give a score to each item.
- Repeat the exercise for every other criterion. If you have x criteria, you will have to perform the pair-ranking exercise x number of times.
- Now pair-rank the various criteria – e.g. cost vs. availability, cost vs. warranty, etc.
- Determine the ranking (relative importance) of the selection criteria.

- Pick three or four of the most important criteria and allocate a relative weighting to each. Ensure that the sum of the weights comes to one.
- Construct a matrix with all the items listed down the first column. In all the other columns list the pair-ranked scores for each criterion.
- Multiply each pair-ranked score by the weighting attributed to that criterion and sum the results across the columns to arrive at a final score.
- The final score will give the overall ranking.

An example of how to carry out a weighted ranking exercise is given in the body of the main text in the section entitled S - Select in Part 2.

Conclusion

I need problems. A good problem makes me come alive

–'Tiny' Rowland

Problem solving is like fitness – the more you practise, the better you will get. Unfortunately many people are afraid of tackling problems and therefore they struggle to get over the first hurdle. However, if you can start the ball rolling, your confidence will grow and grow until eventually you are regarded as an expert problem solver by your colleagues. It may even help in countering the effects of the Peter Principle!

As my last piece of advice, a few bullet points to remember:
- Problem solving is no different to other areas of human effort. Your attitude will largely determine your success. Remain positive and optimistic and do not doubt your problem-solving ability. Avoid cynical and negative people who tend to undermine enthusiasm and creativity.
- Never lose your sense of humour.
- Don't look for solutions before you fully understand the problem.
- There are no set formulae for problem solving. A number of techniques are useful depending on the circumstances. Using your intuition is perhaps the only universal approach or secret, just don't let it become your only method.
- There are many different ways of looking at a problem.
- Don't assume anything. Very often things are not what they seem. Take time to establish the facts.
- Use a combination of logic and intuition.
- Be patient and don't let time pressures dictate your conclusions. You won't solve complex problems immediately and they won't disappear if you apply a sub-optimal solution. Haste affects your overall perspective causing you to overlook opportunities.
- Don't let complexity get you down. Most problems can be reduced to a set of manageable steps that can be taken one at a time.
- Don't take a decision when you're in an emotional state.
- Apply Occam's Razor – choose simplicity over complexity. A brilliant solution that only a few can understand won't be properly implemented.

- The more problems you tackle, the better you will get at solving them.
- Recognise every problem as an opportunity to improve a situation that will lead to unrealised discoveries.
- Don't assume that every difficult problem is a wicked problem. Most problems are tame.
- And as a final 'off-the-wall' piece of advice, keep fit! You'll feel better about yourself.

CIGARS IN SHORT

Circumstances
- Look for the facts – distinguish from the emotions. Observe what is going on.
- Take a helicopter perspective.
- Outside as well as inside opinions – don't rely on one source of information.
- Focus on the key issues (80:20 rule).
- Summarise the circumstances in bullet form.

Impediment
- Define the problem – then redefine it five times.
- Write it down as succinctly as possible.
- Check that it is the core impediment and not a symptom of something else.

Goal
- Define your goal.
- Is the goal related to the impediment?
- Short-term goals are more important than medium or long-term ones.

Alternatives
- Divergent thinking.
- Brainstorm as many alternatives as possible – the more the better.
- Crazy as well as logical solutions – no criticism.
- Consider the impediment and the goal when generating alternatives.

Review
- Convergent thinking. Analyse the merits of each alternative.
- Group similar ideas under a common descriptor.
- Consider practicality of the original ideas. How could they be made to work?
- Reduce the list of possible alternatives to around five.

Select
- Perform weighted ranking with agreed selection criteria.
- Check whether the selected solution feels intuitively correct.
- Develop the implementation plan and assign responsibilities.
- Monitor progress on a regular basis and measure results.

Readers seeking assistance in the implementation of the techniques described in this book may contact the author via the website:

www.closecigar.com

References

1. Allison, M. 1993. *The Problem Buster's Guide*, Gower, Aldershot.

2. Buzan, T. 1988. *Make the Most of Your Mind*, Pan Books, London.

3. Foster, J. 1996. *How To Get Ideas*, Berrett-Koehler Publishers, San Francisco.

4. Foster, T. 1991. *101 Ways To Generate Great Ideas*, Kogan Page, London.

5. Gladwell, M. 2005. *Blink: The Power of Thinking Without Thinking*, Little, Brown and Company, New York.

6. Handy, C. 1994. *The Age of Paradox*, Harvard Business School Press, Boston.

7. Higgins, J M. 1994. *101 Creative Problem Solving Techniques*, New Management Publishing, Florida.

8. Jones, M D. 1995. *The Thinker's Toolkit: Fourteen Powerful Techniques for Problem Solving*, Three Rivers Press, New York.

9. Michalko, M. 1991. *Thinkertoys: A Handbook of Business Creativity*, Ten Speed Press, Berkeley.

10. Rittel, H. & Webber, M. 1973. *Dilemmas in a General Theory of Planning*, Elsevier Scientific Publishing Company, Amsterdam.

11. Surowiecki, J. 2004. *The Wisdom of Crowds: Why the Many Are Smarter Than the Few and How the Collective Wisdom Shapes Business, Economies, Societies and Nations*, Little, Brown and Company, London.

12. Wujec, T. 1995. *Five Star Mind: Games and Exercises to Stimulate Your Creativity and Imagination*, Doubleday, New York.

www.ingramcontent.com/pod-product-compliance
Lightning Source LLC
Chambersburg PA
CBHW021957170526
45157CB00003B/1035